PRINCE PHILIP

PRINCE PHILIP
THE DUKE OF EDINBURGH

AN ILLUSTRATED BIOGRAPHY

Michael Paterson

CONSTABLE • LONDON

This book is dedicated to two dear friends
ALAN AND TANIS BARROW
and to my colleagues at Eton
REB HUNKIN, ANNE COWARD and CHARLOTTE VILLIERS

I am extremely grateful to two Charlottes – Charlotte Macdonald at Constable & Robinson who asked me to write the text, and Charlotte Cole who then edited it. Both have been absolutely delightful to work with, and made this project even more enjoyable. I also thank Peter McMullen-Bell and Barry Marsh – they will know why – and, as always, Sarah.

Constable & Robinson Ltd
55–56 Russell Square, London WC1B 4HP
www.constablerobinson.com

First published in the UK in 2013 by Constable,
an imprint of Constable & Robinson Ltd, in association with the Daily Mail

A copy of the British Library Cataloguing in Publication Data is available from the British Library

UK ISBN: 978-1-47211-256-9 (hardback)

Designed by Design 23, London
Printed and bound in Italy

CONTENTS

PREFACE

The Field of Remembrance, Westminster Abbey. It is the usual grey November day and the crowd, both military and civilian, is well wrapped up against the chill as it awaits his arrival to inspect the neat rows of plots. Each one, marked off by a border of balsawood or plastic crosses, commemorates a unit – a regiment, a corps, a squadron, a ship's company or an old comrades' association. Within every designated space there are more of the little crosses. These bear the names of individuals. There are thousands of them, though they are not evenly distributed. With some of the bigger regiments, such as the Royal Artillery, they crowd so thickly that the grass can hardly be seen. Others have very few.

From the roof of St Margaret's church there is a flash of gold State Dress and a long, swelling trumpet fanfare. It is the signal that he is here. The crowd, intent on its own conversations, did not notice his arrival, but suddenly there is a big, official-looking car at the kerb. Dignitaries are crowding by the gate, a huge RAF sergeant and his superior – a tiny female officer – snap brisk salutes and he appears, followed by a gaggle of others. He walks slowly, and with a stoop,

shoulders hunched, looking to left and right. He is wearing the uniform of a senior naval officer – a greatcoat and cap – and as he comes nearer you notice how well-worn it is. He has been an Admiral of the Fleet for sixty years – much longer than any ordinary person could hold such a rank – and the gold wire on his cap and shoulder boards is dulled and frayed. Beneath the black visor and the shaggy brows, however, his blue eyes are bright, watchful, sometimes curious, sometimes even showing a twinkle of amusement. More often they are glassy with disinterest.

He looks at some plots and ignores others. It could not really be otherwise, for there are dozens of them and his time is limited. He stops to exchange a few syllables with those who for one reason or another are conspicuous – a Chelsea Pensioner in scarlet, a naval petty officer, a man whose blazer is sagging under the weight of medals. He points at things here and there, muttering brief questions. Everyone remains at attention as he passes – you can sense the crowd holding its breath – and each plot has at the front of it an officer, or some other functionary, who is ready to inform should His Royal Highness show an interest. One man thinks that the trick is to call out the name as he passes. If you say, loudly and cheerfully: 'Royal Blankshire Fusiliers, sir!' or 'Legion of Frontiersmen!' or 'Salonika Association, sir!' it may cause him to stop and come over.

It works. He glances over the man's shoulder at the thin scattering of wooden markers, reads the title on its cardboard placard, and then looks him in the eye. 'Not many of them,' he remarks. 'No, sir.' 'At least that means,' he says, gruffly, 'that there'll be room for yours when you go!' He barks a short laugh and is gone.

Some of those present found this rude. Others thought it funny, and that is often the way with Prince Philip. Some consider his directness, especially if his remarks are delivered in a sarcastic tone or without a smile, insensitive. Others enjoy his blunt sense of humour, his ability to entertain and to lighten the atmosphere even in solemn surroundings, his conforming to their expectations, providing them with an anecdote that they can relate afterwards over a pint. For every one who finds his manner offensive there seem to be ten who revere him. As the crowd disperses in his wake a burly regimental sergeant major, who served with the Grenadier Guards – Philip's regiment – smiles. 'I *love* the man!' he says.

PREVIOUS SPREAD:
TOP LEFT: The Duke of Edinburgh, as Senior Colonel of the Household Division, pins the South Atlantic Medal on Guardsman Simon Weston, at Buckingham Palace. Guardsman Weston was wounded during the Falklands War.

BOTTOM LEFT: Prince Philip examines a badge worn by Cecil McKee from Belfast, during a reception for the Corps of Commissionaires, in honour of their 150th anniversary, at St James's Palace.

RIGHT: The Queen and Prince Philip prior to the Queens Company Review at Windsor Castle.

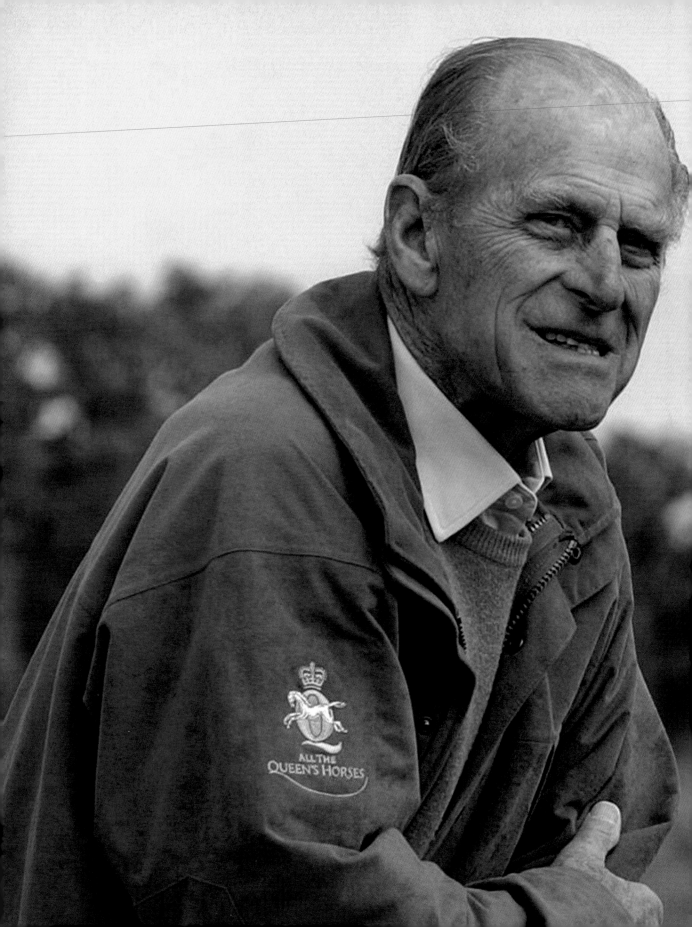

CHAPTER ONE

THE MOST INTERESTING MAN IN BRITAIN

PREVIOUS SPREAD: Prince Philip during a tour of battlefields in the Crimea, Ukraine, 2004.

LEFT: The Queen and Prince Philip, wearing the uniform of an Admiral of the Fleet, in Buckingham Palace after the State Opening of Parliament, 1972.

Prince Philip is not only the longest-serving consort in British history (he married Princess Elizabeth in 1947; she became Queen in 1952) but surely – and by a considerable margin – the most interesting man in Britain. He has been a prince, then a commoner, then a duke and then once again a prince. He has been a professional naval officer and an amateur sportsman, the patron of numerous charitable organizations and the extremely active head of several. He holds the highest positions in the Navy, Army and Air Force and is colonel-in-chief of several regiments (including in turn two of the Foot Guards, the Welsh and the Grenadiers). He is a qualified pilot of both helicopters and fixed-wing craft. He is an accomplished sailor who has competed in yacht races. He has been a keen cricketer and an even more enthusiastic polo player. He has put one sport – carriage-driving – on the map entirely through his participation in it, and he even once threw the javelin in naval sporting competitions. He is a painter of genuine talent. He has travelled the earth, climbed down mines and up mountains, met virtually every significant head of state or prime minister in the world, and yet he has never lost the 'common touch'. His cousin, Queen Alexandra of Yugoslavia, wrote of him in a biography that he 'has walked at the head of the stately procession of the Order of the Garter and slaved half-naked in the stokehold of a troop-ship. He knows what it is to eat steak and chips in sleazy seaport cafés and what it is to be repeatedly the applauded guest of honour at a crowded Guildhall banquet.'

He is one of the country's most accomplished public speakers, and has an enviable ability to talk to people in all situations. He is knowledgeable, intelligent and so witty that books have been published about his humorous remarks. He can be droll, spontaneous and very funny. When his youngest son, Prince Edward, applied to Cambridge University, it was highly likely that less-than-impressive A-level results would hinder his chances. However, because admission is a matter of acceptance by an individual college rather than by the university, there was a possibility that some well-disposed admissions tutor would have him, and this indeed happened. There was palpable relief in Edward's family when one establishment, Jesus College, made an offer. 'What a friend we have in Jesus!' quipped Prince Philip (another version has him saying: 'Thank God for Jesus!').

Sometimes, perhaps more often than we realize, his victims retort. Once, at a reception in Brasilia, he was introduced to an admiral who was bedecked with medals. These included one for service in the Second World War – in which Brazil had played a very minor role. Philip grunted: 'I didn't know Brazil was in the war that long,' to which the man replied huffily: 'At least, sir, I didn't get them from marrying my wife.'

He has enough sense of humour to appreciate – depending on his mood – such comebacks. Anyone who knows him will tell you that he is self-deprecating to a fault. He enjoys humour at his own expense, providing it is actually funny and he can see the joke. After all, for decades he has collected press cartoons about himself. There must by now be enough of them, framed on the walls of his various dressing-rooms and corridors and lavatories, to fill a whole art gallery. The public have of course seen these too on the pages of their newspapers. Perhaps the most apt of them all was produced a number of years ago, when he was known to be keen on both birdwatching and photography. He travelled to exotic places, recording the wildlife (and produced a book called *Birds from Britannia*). The picture shows him, on the Galapagos Islands or somewhere, about to snap nesting albatrosses. One bird looks indignantly at another and snaps: 'Bloody photographers!' – a comment he has himself made more than once. He would have liked that.

In conversation he can be friendly, even familiar, but he expects always to be addressed as 'Sir' and as 'Your Royal Highness'. Any informality during an encounter will be initiated by him but it is definitely not an invitation to respond in kind, and that is as it should be. As for his outspokenness, he is of course not as insensitive as he seems. He knows better than anyone that any remark that is

TOP RIGHT: Prince Philip takes a photograph with his Hasselblad camera.

BOTTOM RIGHT: Prince Philip keeps his thumb on the button as he tries the facilities with a hearing test, during a visit to the Royal National Institute for Deaf People in London.

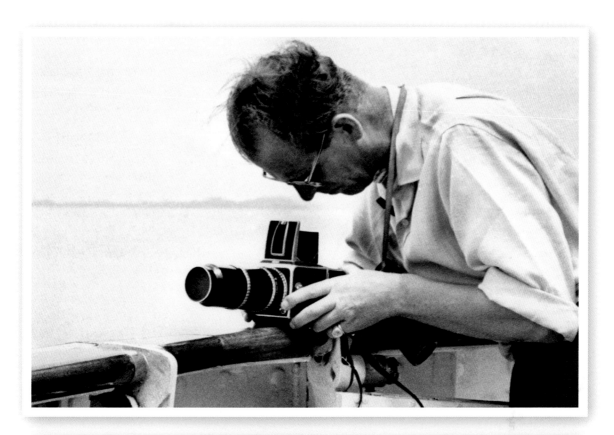

TOP LEFT: Prince Philip talks to Aboriginal performers after watching a culture show at Tjapukai Aboriginal Culture Park, Cairns, Queensland, Australia.

BOTTOM LEFT: Prince Philip and Dr Kwame Nkrumah, President of Ghana, share a joke centred round the latter's walking stick, while Princess Anne looks on, in the grounds of Balmoral Castle.

thoughtless, or can be interpreted as offensive, will be all over the following day's newspapers.

He is routinely quoted out of context. Such is the press fixation with his utterances that reporters who follow him are visibly longing for him to slip up – especially abroad, where he is expected to be a particular source of embarrassment. His enquiry when talking to an Australian Aborigine: 'Do you still throw spears at each other?' is the sort of thing that today's media is unlikely to overlook or to forget. As so often, the person who was actually asked the question did not find it offensive, for this native people jealously preserves its traditions and these include the weapons – spears and boomerangs – with which they have hunted for millennia. Perhaps his most infamous remark was in China, where he met young British people who were studying there and told them that if they stayed too long in the country they'd go 'slitty-eyed'. No one took the trouble to point out that he was simply turning on its head a common Chinese saying, which is that members of that race who spend too long in the West will go 'round-eyed'. He let the storm blow itself out. To argue would simply open the wound even deeper. Nevertheless, he has been quoted as lamenting that; 'There's [sic] an awful lot of things that, if I were to re-read them now, I'd say to myself: Good God, I wish I hadn't said that!'

It's worth remembering that he came into public life comparatively young, and that he has been obliged to make many hundreds of speeches and hold millions of conversations since then. He will have said things on the spur of the moment, when tired or irritated or unprepared, and then suffered because these throwaway conversations were preserved in print or passed on by word of mouth. Mistakes are not forgotten, they are collected together and published in books, and that is unfair on anyone – even if, in some cases, the proceeds have benefited his charities. Naturally he is not perfect.

Occasional stories give the impression that his bad temper is notorious among royal servants, journalists and members of the public, but it is the anger not of a naturally malicious personality but of someone who has great responsibility and who has to be able to depend on others doing things well, or on them having the courtesy not to provoke him with stupid or impertinent questions.

It is worth remembering that, though he is impatient and bad-tempered with those around him who fail in some important way (and they need not even belong to the human race. Anyone who saw him taking part in carriage-driving contests will remember how he used to swear at the horses!), he is equally self-critical when the fault is his. 'I get just as angry with myself if I make a mistake or do something silly,' he has said.

He loves the Armed Forces not only because they represent an environment that is comfortable and familiar but, because he is at the top of this very hierarchical body, he can expect both complete discretion and a respect that will be absolute – without being in the least fawning.

He is indeed much respected by members of the Forces, and not least for a reason given earlier: he has experienced the life they lead at first hand. He was a serving naval officer throughout the Second World War and saw action – he undertook risky convoy duty and gained a mention in despatches at the Battle of Cape Matapan. He has earned his wings in the RAF like any other pilot. He has been colonel-in-chief, an honorary position, of several regiments and has, despite advanced age, visited them even in theatres of conflict.

Many both inside and outside the Services greatly admire his decisive, no-nonsense, plain-spoken nature. Others, especially women, appreciate the way in which he has supported the Queen through the long years of her reign, providing her with an invaluable confidant and sharing so many of the tasks she performs. To those who revere tradition and duty and discipline, to those of a socially conservative, perhaps even a reactionary, bent, he is a hero and a national treasure. Small wonder that when, in 1969, a Gallup poll asked the public who would make the best dictator of a British totalitarian state, he received the most votes. If he had been a person of lesser ability, he could have

RIGHT: Princess Elizabeth and Lieutenant Philip Mountbatten pose for their first engagement pictures at Buckingham Palace.

TOP LEFT: Prince Philip
at his desk in Buckingham
Palace.

BOTTOM LEFT: Prince
Philip, who had been
'signed up' by Anglia
Television to co-host Peter
Scott's documentary on
wildlife conservation called
It's Now or Never, seen on
location in Africa.

BOTTOM RIGHT: Prince
Philip, in uniform as
Admiral of the Fleet,
in the Throne Room of
Buckingham Palace, after
the Coronation of Queen
Elizabeth II, on 2 June.

been an embarrassment to the Royal Family. As it is, he has so clearly earned his way and deserved the privileges that go with his position that it is difficult not to respect him.

He is undoubtedly more flexible, and more independent, than the Queen could afford to be. While she will dutifully co-operate with those whose task is to ensure her safety, he has always chafed irritably at his protection officers. They know that they must stay as far from him as efficiency and professionalism will permit, for he does not want to see them or feel their presence. He has, in fact, been able to achieve a surprising amount of anonymity, for some years ago he acquired his own London taxi and is able to use this to slip unnoticed through the streets of the capital when going to and from engagements.

His longevity is astonishing. Though he is one of thousands of Second World War veterans still living, he is the only one who remains vitally involved in the life of the nation at a high level. It is remarkable – and virtually unheard of outside the Royal Family – that anyone still in public life should have taken part in wartime battles, or indeed been to Nazi Germany. He was a frequent visitor to his relatives there – in 1937 he went to West Germany for the funeral of his sister Cecile and brother-in-law, where another who attended was Hermann Göring. To have been to a place that, mercifully, seems almost too remote in history to imagine, and to have shared an experience with such a historical villain, yet to be actively involved in the everyday doings of modern Britain makes him a bridge between past and present, a living historical monument.

Similarly, it seems astonishing that he was one of the people who designed Britain's decimal currency – he was at the time president of the advisory committee at the Royal Mint that dealt with this challenge – for it is the only coinage a large number of his wife's subjects have ever used. Like the Queen, he has been there throughout the entire lives of millions of Britons. Like Her Majesty, he has never adjusted his appearance according to changes in fashion, and thus has about him the same quality of timelessness.

The most memorable outbursts of temper in public — and there are fewer of these in any case as he has got older — have been caused by what he sees as mistreatment of the Queen: badly made arrangements that cause her inconvenience, or stupid and impertinent questions from journalists. That he becomes angry on her behalf is an attractive trait, for he is extremely — and touchingly — protective of her.

They are wonderfully suited to operating as a team, a balance of qualities and strengths that help them to function effectively. When they meet the public he provides the light relief, she the unwavering dignity. He asks the chatty questions, and points out to her people in the crowd who merit attention or who are visibly desperate to be seen by her. At Williamsburg, Virginia, he spotted a small boy who was longing to present a bouquet but was discouraged by a line of police tape and the presence of several state troopers, whose job was naturally to stop anyone getting near the Queen. Philip, at his most avuncular, waved the boy forward and saw him safely across the road. The Queen was happy to meet him, and the young man himself seemed to be walking on air as he returned. With so much experience of 'walkabouts', he is consummate in handling people. If it is a very big crowd, he may decide to stop and talk to every tenth person. If it is smaller, it could be every third. But he is flexible, of course, and will in any case be keeping an eye out for anyone unusual. He will not always feel confrontational — one young man who was at a camp he visited said afterwards, 'Prince Philip spoke to the boy next to me on two occasions but I was just stared at and ignored.' He then added, 'Maybe it was my hammer and sickle badge …' Philip also uses humour to break the ice. Knowing that many people are tongue-tied in the presence of royalty, he will make one bystander laugh in order to put all the others at their ease. Some of the laughter may be forced, but it is still preferable to silence. Philip has always been good at these things.

His great strength has been incisively summed up by one of his biographers, Basil Boothroyd: 'He goes where the Queen can't go, meets people she can't meet, does things she can't do, hears things she

can't hear – and brings it all back: not only to particularize, with all the up-link data on fruit imports, afforestation, the armed forces, drug addiction, fishing rights, Finland, the state of the Church, or what you will, but as a fountain of general knowledge about the country and the world that a king and queen between them couldn't acquire.' Writers about the Queen have referred to the fact that, because she and Philip often have separate commitments, Her Majesty enjoys sitting at home late in the evenings when her husband returns from some function or other and hearing all about it. They share a sense of humour, and will undoubtedly be able to laugh over any absurdities in whatever situation he describes. He is the most useful of confidants and advisors, and vicariously he can add a whole dimension to her experience. He has been her eyes and ears for decades, ever since they were married.

The fact that he has had such wide interests and pursued them with such energy and dedication has been an inspiration to the rest of us. That he remains so active when in his nineties – and it is his exceptional physical and mental health that has enabled him to do this – is also inspirational. He announced, on reaching his tenth decade, that he had now 'done his bit', and would undertake a great deal less in the way of public duties. Nevertheless he still carried out 347 of these during 2012 – and that was actually an increase on the 330 in 2011. A few years previously, in 2007, the Danish journalist Trine Villemann recorded that her country's 29-year-old Crown Prince, Frederik, carried out seventy public engagements in the course of the twelve months. She compared this with Prince Philip, who at the time was 86 and whose tally was 380. This total, she added, did not include such things as private briefings or meetings of the privy council, so that he is even more hard-working than he seemed. In previous years, when he had more energy, he would reply to suggestions that he slow down or curtail his programme – in the way that Diana was to do – by saying, 'What would I do – sit and knit?'

In these engagements, as in everything he has done for so long, he has been superbly efficient. As his friend Gyles Brandreth observed in 2012, at a time when Prince Philip was hospitalized during the Diamond Jubilee celebrations: 'In sixty years he has never been late, never gone to the wrong address, never dressed in the wrong uniform and there have been five occasions in all that time when he has cried off because of illness.' That latter total has since increased, but the point is well worth making, and this is an impressive summary of his contribution to national life. Granted that he has staff to lay out the uniforms and to convey him to his appointments, he still has the not inconsiderable task of understanding why he is there, looking and sounding interested in whatever is shown him, and often making a speech that may well be published and which must therefore strike the right note. A photograph once showed him, dressed in a lab coat, visiting the Scottish factory that makes Baxters soups. He was tasting a spoonful of one of them. The caption noted that his expression was carefully neutral, since any look of displeasure could be worth a fortune to competitors. The rest of us do not think of these things because we don't have to. He must always be aware of a scrutiny that can be partisan.

Though he cannot vote and does not express political views, it is safe to assume that his stance on most things is to the right of centre and it would be surprising, all things considered, if it were anything else. Asked by the left-wing journalist Polly Toynbee if he ever read the *Guardian*, he expostulated 'No Fear!' It was widely held in the seventies that his uncle, Lord Mountbatten (a man who – despite a background of blue blood and a marked personal snobbery – actually did hold left-wing views), sent Philip a subscription to the *New Statesman* every year as a joke, though it is not known what he did with the copies when they arrived. It would, however, be doing him a major injustice to assume that the only company he enjoys is that of naval officers or fellow grouse-shooters. He gets on extremely well with creative people – he is one himself, after all – and his interests are much wider than caricature would suggest. Indeed he was appionted President of the Royal Society of Arts. Some might be surprised to learn that he was

TOP RIGHT: The Queen and Prince Philip watch a presentation during a visit to the *Cutty Sark* in Greenwich, London, 2012.

BOTTOM RIGHT: Prince Philip and Queen Elizabeth II during the third day of the Royal Windsor Horse show, in Windsor, 2013.

TOP LEFT: The Queen accompanied by Prince Philip during the official re-opening of Baxter Park and pavilion in Dundee, 2007.

BOTTOM LEFT: The Queen and Philip chat while seated during a musical performance in the Abbey Gardens, Bury St Edmunds, during her Golden Jubilee visit to Suffolk.

one of the moving spirits in establishing the Design Centre. Though the actual founder was a man called Gordon Russell who was himself a designer, it was the personal interest that Philip took in this notion – of a showcase for new design and for a body that would provide a seal of excellence for products (something that the public has overwhelmingly come to trust) – that really got it off the ground. Australia too has an annual design award named after him.

This sort of worthy gesture – taking an interest in modern design and dishing out awards for it – is very much the sort of thing for which Queen Victoria's husband, Prince Albert (1819–61), was known. Comparisons between Philip and his predecessor Albert have been made since the moment he became engaged to Princess Elizabeth, and he famously does not like them – although before and after his wedding he read extensively about the life and work of Victoria's husband. There was some initial common ground. Both men were poor by royal standards, and were seen by cynics as adventurers, marrying into wealth. Both would have had little scope in their home countries, and both were subject to initial public suspicion. Both were highly intelligent and both worked extremely hard as patrons, as promoters of science, industry and technology. Philip has never, however, adopted Albert's practice of going through his wife's dispatch boxes with her. He would never have been allowed to do this, even if he had wanted to. The situation in Victoria's reign was entirely different, for the arrangements she inherited were looser and business was carried out in a less structured manner. She had no private secretary to advise her. Albert, the man she trusted most, filled a void in royal administration that no longer exists, thanks to an efficient and well-trained professional staff. Philip has a diary filled with his own activities, and he scrupulously avoids interference in the Queen's business.

The personalities of the two men are also extremely unalike. Albert was a quiet and studious man whose earnestness was his most noticeable characteristic, whereas Philip's would be, perhaps, humour and social ease. Their backgrounds were very different. Albert had been brought up in effective isolation, educated by tutors in a secluded minor German court. Philip lived on terms of equality with schoolboys and sailors for years before becoming a public figure. Albert, though he shot (very badly!), never took an interest in sports. When shown a cricket match in progress one afternoon, he marvelled disapprovingly at the idleness of the fielders as they stood about waiting for the batsman to send a ball over. He could not imagine why young men were encouraged to waste their time on such an activity. Philip, of course, not only excelled at England's national game but has enjoyed a number of others. He has shot, sailed, flown, driven carriages, played polo and hockey. Albert never journeyed outside Europe while Philip, living in an age of much easier travel, has been all over the world. Albert had no great feeling for the Armed Forces (though he sought to design more practical uniforms for soldiers) while Philip is entirely in his element with them. Albert was almost bereft of humour, and certainly would not have matched Philip's comfortable manner in talking to the public (though to be fair there would in Albert's case have been no question of encountering them on such an informal basis) let alone making them laugh. One could not imagine Victoria's husband making the quip, as Philip did when meeting a man who told him, 'My wife is a doctor of philosophy, and much more important than I am': 'Yes, we have that trouble in our family too!' And nor would Albert have raised blushes among a crowd, as Philip did when, shortly after he and the Princess were married, someone remarked on the purity of her complexion. 'Yes,' he replied, 'and she's like that all over!'

A more apt comparison with a fellow consort is perhaps a recent case in a neighbouring country. Prince Bernhard of the Netherlands (1911–2004) was the husband of Queen Juliana. A German prince who married into the House of Orange in 1937, Bernhard swiftly became a national figure in his adopted country. He was young, intelligent, immensely versatile and energetic. He rapidly identified fields of both work and leisure that he could make his own, and gained popularity as something of a daredevil. He was to become respected

TOP RIGHT: The Queen and Philip in Rotorua, New Zealand, during her Silver Jubilee tour.

BOTTOM RIGHT: Philip jumps ashore from the Royal Forth Yacht Club vessel *The Royal Forth* after a tour of Granton Harbour, Edinburgh.

LEFT: Prince Philip during
his visit to the Kahna
Forest Game Reserve on
the fourth day of the Royal
Tour of India, 1983.

by the army and by military veterans, for he acted as aide de camp to
his mother-in-law Queen Wilhelmina in the war, and she afterwards
awarded him the nation's highest medal for valour. He took a keen
interest in the navy, and like Philip he was an enthusiastic amateur
pilot. He was associated with fast cars, show-jumping, fighter aircraft
(he served as a pilot in the expatriate Dutch Air Force) and skiing. Yet
he also headed a number of charitable organizations and, like Philip,
was to serve as President of the World Wildlife Fund. He filled, in the
life of the Netherlands, precisely the function – that of role-model
for youth, followed by middle-aged symbol of stability and then
grandfather of the nation – that Prince Philip has in Britain, and even
had a similarly gruff sense of humour. They were the only two men
in the world who had so much in common with each other, and both
modernized the image of their countries' monarchies and made them
exciting and accessible.

Like the Queen, the Duke has enjoyed enviable good health
throughout his life. He has never had a serious illness. Most people are
unaware that he has for decades been short-sighted and that he wears
glasses, though he does not like to do so in public. Similarly, many are
shocked by the frequency with which he now seems to go into hospital
(he has been four times in five years, and a rumour that he suffers from
prostate cancer has been denied). At the time of writing this book, in
the summer of 2013, several people have told the present author, 'You
may not finish it in time' or, 'You'd better hurry up with it while he's
still here' – such is the image of robust health he has always projected
that what are common ailments in a man his age suggest to some that
he is nearing the end of his life. The fact is that he is remarkably fit for a
man in his nineties. He remained an athlete of sorts until his seventies,
and did himself the favour of giving up smoking when in his twenties.
He has access to expert medical care whenever he needs it. Might he
not reach a hundred and receive an official greeting from the Queen, as
his mother-in-law did?

In his blunt and no-nonsense way he tends to brush aside praise.

He has referred to himself as an 'uncultured, polo-playing clot', an 'ignorant bum' and 'a mine of useless information'. He has dismissed his artistic abilities as 'strictly average' and said of his war record that 'there are hundreds upon thousands of records just like it'. He has also commented that, 'I doubt whether I've achieved anything likely to be remembered.' Despite this modesty he has, from the beginning of his life, been notable for an overwhelming self-assurance. This has been of immeasurable value to the country, for it has enabled him to do so much that has been useful, whether talking to visiting heads of state or providing the initiative for charity fundraising. Where does this confidence come from?

First of all, he was born male in a family of girls. Philip was the youngest child – and only son – of his parents. In Greek culture a boy was, and still is, considered of far greater importance than a girl. In a royal family, a male child will have been of even greater importance for, although he was only sixth in the line of succession after his father and uncles, he nevertheless represented for monarchists the future of Greece. That he had four older sisters will have meant that he was indulged from the beginning – even though they stated in later life that they had gone to great lengths not to spoil him, and indeed claimed that they had been deliberately disagreeable, for his own good. An intelligent and outgoing child inclined to mischief, his misdemeanours will have been tolerated and his position at the centre of the family will have been secure. Philip was not only looked after by sisters but by a virtual army of aunts, uncles, cousins and grandparents.

Secondly, he was part of a royal family. Though the ruling house of Greece was a minor and a young monarchy and the country unstable – the family had to flee abroad months after his birth – he was nevertheless part of a network of important and well-known people who occupied thrones, and who lived in palaces and castles. His relations were people with wealth, power, prestige, possessions – he belonged to a family with the resounding name of Schleswig-Holstein-

TOP LEFT: Philip batting during the 12-a-side cricket match between the Duke of Edinburgh and the Duke of Norfolk. His team was made up of former England cricketers, and the Duke of Norfolk's mainly Sussex players.

TOP RIGHT: Philip, with his left arm bandaged, as he returned from practice at Cowdray Park before playing for Windsor Park against the Brazilian team Sao Silvestre.

BOTTOM: Prince Charles and Princess Anne being pushed on a swing by their father, with their mother looking on, in the grounds of Balmoral.

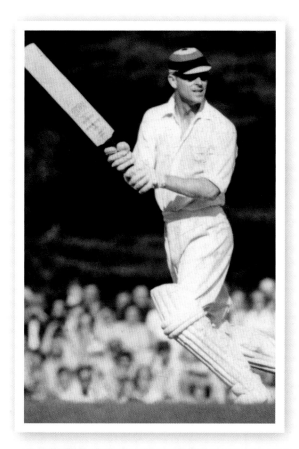

TOP: Charles with his
father Philip and crew
members Uffa Fox,
the Duke's yachting
adviser, and Lieutenant-
Commander Alistair
Easton, Sailing Master
of the yacht *Bluebottle*,
at Cowes, during their
Dragon-Class race.

BOTTOM: Philip
conducting ashore Crown
Prince Olav, Crown
Princess Marta and
Princess Astrid (behind)
at Westminster Pier when
they arrived to represent
King Haakon VII of Norway
at the Coronation.

Sonderburg-Glücksburg, and was a Prince of Greece and Denmark. As
a member of this class he would be saluted by policemen and deferred
to by servants and courtiers. He would, from the time he emerged
from childhood, if not before, have been viewed as a potential husband
for the young women who shared this background.

He would in other words have been accustomed, from earliest
consciousness, to both the respect and the curiosity of others. He
would have taken for granted the grandest of surroundings, for while
throughout his childhood and youth he did not live in a palace he
certainly stayed in such places as a guest of his relations, as well as in
country houses and elegant town residences.

Thirdly, he had excellent mentors. These included his school
headmaster, the educationalist Dr Kurt Hahn, but by far the most
important was his uncle, Lord Louis Mountbatten (1900–79).
Mountbatten was more than just a kind and helpful uncle, or even – as
he undoubtedly was – a role model. He had an agenda of his own. A
man of overwhelming ambition, he wanted the minor German royal
house to which he and Philip belonged (the Battenbergs, anglicized
to Mountbatten during the First World War) to achieve much greater
status and prestige. In the space of a few years, Mountbatten saw
in his nephew a means of achieving this, as the boy emerged from
adolescence into young manhood just in time to be caught up in the
Second World War.

Philip attracted such interest because he deserved it. He had genuine
ability. As a cadet in the Navy and as a young officer he fulfilled all the
hopes of those who had spent on him their time and trouble. His uncle
was delighted – and probably flattered – that Philip wanted to follow
him into the Navy. Philip was promising enough to advance on his own
merits, and his progress will have been a source of pride. Similarly, it was
Mountbatten who first wanted him to marry the British King's daughter,
Princess Elizabeth. Yet no amount of cajoling or arranging could have
made the two young people fond of each other, much less created the
successful marriage that has lasted the rest of their lives.

Fourthly, Philip had a natural intellect. He was to bring to Britain's royal family a degree of intelligence it had not known since the days of the other great consort, Prince Albert. Philip was not an academic but he possessed a deep interest in technology and a sincere curiosity about 'how things work' that were to identify him with the scientific age in which he has lived. His understanding of this field would impress experts and allow him to be unfazed by serving in such 'egghead' offices as chancellor of universities (Cambridge, Edinburgh, Wales) and President of the British Association for the Advancement of Science. Together with this enthusiasm he has exhaustively wide interests. As one biographer, General Sir Leslie Hollis, wrote: 'Greater minds than mine have called attention to his quick grasp of any new subject and his keen and genuine interest in so many sides of life.' Royalty has always been able to ask polite questions or offer encouragement. Philip was also able to interrogate, to comprehend and to challenge. His ability here has won unstinted admiration.

Fifthly, and most obviously, Philip grew up to be as handsome as a film star. He reached six foot two and had steel-blue eyes, a slim and muscular build, and a boyish mop of white-blond hair. He set hearts fluttering all over Europe. More attractive than any other member of his family, including his sons and grandsons, he had the natural confidence that can only be experienced by those of such striking looks. As if this were not enough, he also had extremely good manners. Today he is known for a bluff and sometimes cantankerous exterior, but he has always had considerable charm, as well as a genuine consideration for others, that has won over some of his critics. Even as a small boy he was punctilious in thanking others for kindnesses.

RIGHT: Philip after presenting campaign medals to members of 40 Commando who have completed their first tour of Afghanistan, at Norton Manor Camp, Somerset, following their return.

CHAPTER TWO

A TRULY
EUROPEAN ROYAL

Apart from being a great-great-grandson of Queen Victoria – whose name still, when he was born just over twenty years after her death, resonated throughout Europe – Philip is a descendant of a gentleman called Christian the Warlike, who became Count of Oldenburg (a territory in the German–Danish lands near the Baltic Sea) in the early twelfth century and who founded a house that was to dominate that corner of Europe.

Philip's grandfather, King George I of Greece (1845–1913), had started life as a Danish prince called William and had gone into the Navy as a career officer. When he was seventeen, however, a delegation from Athens had asked him to assume the throne of a country whose language he could not speak, about whose affairs he knew nothing – and whose corrupt and complex political establishment he could not hope to dominate. Nevertheless he tried, and proved a conscientious sovereign. His wife, a Russian princess whom he had chosen and courted with almost alarming speed, shared with him the popularity he attained with his people. They had eight children. Prince Andrew ('Andrea' to the family) was the second youngest.

Prince Andrew would grow up to be tall and strikingly handsome, exhibiting some of the physical characteristics – piercing eyes, a strong brow and chin – that his son would inherit. He was educated for the Army, his training consisting of an exaggeratedly rigorous version of the military school course, and was commissioned into the cavalry. His brothers, including the eldest, Crown Prince Constantine, were in the Army too. In 1903 Andrew married Princess Alice of Battenberg, whom he had met in London at the coronation of Edward VII. The couple soon began to have children – there would be five in all – and divided their time between palaces, garrisons and visits abroad.

In Greece, however, the monarchy went in and out of popularity. There were frequent assassination attempts against the King, and in March 1913 one of them succeeded. The princes were forced by often savage republican criticism to resign their commissions, and their stature was restored only when national emergencies – in the shape of Balkan wars – made their military skills necessary. When campaigns went well they reaped rewards in public acclaim. When matters went badly they risked becoming scapegoats.

King George had been succeeded by his son Constantine, who in 1917 was forced by the Allies to abdicate after trying unsuccessfully to keep his country neutral in the face of pressure to join them in the Great War. His second son, Alexander, became king but died only three years later after being bitten by a monkey. In 1920 Constantine, back from exile, became king again. The monarchy was popular and so was the notion of war against Turkey to expand national territory. Andrew was put in command of an Army division that struck east through Smyrna and initially drove back the enemy. Early success gave the Greek public an inflated idea of the capabilities of an Army that in reality was badly trained and equipped. Disaster, the result of efficiently led Turkish troops and overstretched Greek supply lines, caused defeat, and Andrew, who had thought the campaign ill-conceived, was to face an opprobrium that would very nearly prove fatal. Government and people were intent on blaming military defeat on bad leadership – and it caused him to lose his country and be sent into permanent exile.

On his mother's side, Philip's ancestry is German–English. By the standards of European royalty they were, however, a minor family and one that had known disgrace. In 1851 Prince Alexander of Hesse-Darmstadt, a younger brother of that state's ruler, had eloped with a woman called Julie Hauke who was a maid of honour to the wife of the Russian Tsesarevich. His family was appalled. So was the Russian Army, from which he had to resign (he went into Austrian service instead). His wife was subject to years of sneers and snubs. She was forbidden to assume the style of princess, but the family did not want a mere 'Frau' among its members. She was therefore created a countess and awarded a title – Battenberg – that

TOP LEFT: Crown Princess Cecilie with Miss Glasgow Mullen at the wedding of John Leighton Barran and Hon Alison Hore-Ruthven at the Guards Chapel, Wellington Barracks. Princess Cecilie of Greece and Denmark was the wife of Hereditary Grand Duke George Donatus of Hesse and the sister of Prince Philip, Duke of Edinburgh.

TOP RIGHT: King Michael of Romania (right) rides with his cousin Prince Philip of Greece on the sands at Constanza.

BOTTOM: Lady Louise Mountbatten with, left, Princess Theodora of Greece and, right, Princess Margarita of Greece, daughters of Prince Andrew of Greece and Denmark, and sisters of Philip.

TOP LEFT: Prince Philip acts as an usher, assisting Princess Elizabeth, right, and Princess Margaret Rose, with their coats as they arrive at Romsey Abbey, Hampshire, 23 December 1946, for the wedding of Patricia Mountbatten.

BOTTOM LEFT: Queen Noor of Jordan (left), the Queen and Prince Philip, and (right) King Hussein of Jordan on the shore of the Dead Sea, on the third day of the state visit to Jordan.

OPPOSITE TOP LEFT: Princess Sophie of Greece, youngest daughter of Prince Andrew of Greece, and sister of Philip.

TOP RIGHT: Princess Alice of Battenberg, widow of Prince Andrew of Greece, Philip's mother.

BOTTOM RIGHT: The family wave goodbye to Viscount Mountbatten, unseen, as he leaves England to become Viceroy of India from Northolt Airport, 1947, with his wife and youngest daughter. Waving goodbye to them from left to right, Lady Doreen Brabourne, Lady Patricia Brabourne, eldest daughter of Viscount Mountbatten, and Philip.

had become defunct. The stigma that attached to her, and which she heroically disregarded, would not pass to later generations; four of her five children were to marry into royal houses, including that of Great Britain. Yet it is possible to see from her experience how some of her descendants would be possessed of a burning desire to enhance the prestige of their family. In none of them would this be more clearly manifest than in Louis Mountbatten.

Some years after her marriage, the countess was promoted after all to princess, enabling her children to have the title prince or princess. One of them was Prince Louis of Battenberg (1854–1921), a highly gifted young man who sought a career at sea, and joined the British Senior Service – becoming a naturalized citizen in order to do so – because no German navy existed at the time. His daughter Alice would be Philip's mother.

During the First World War, public suspicion of Louis' Germanic background forced him to resign his position – a sad irony, for he was one of the chief architects of the modern Navy that had defied Germany in 1914. It was from this part of the family (domiciled in England and British in nationality and feeling, and with the recently anglicized name of Mountbatten) rather than from any Danish connection, that Philip was to derive his character, his nautical passion and his anglophilia. Though Prince Louis died the year Philip was born – his first visit to England, at the age of a few months, was for the prince's funeral – his mother's family provided the two men, her brothers, who would guide him through early life and whose influence would be decisive: George, Marquess of Milford Haven (1892–1938), and Louis Mountbatten (1900–1979). There would be in Philip's nature nothing obviously Greek – he would never learn the language – and nor was there anything especially Danish (he would not learn that one either) except for his striking fair hair.

CHAPTER THREE

EDUCATION AND BOYHOOD

It could not possibly be said that Philip led a sheltered life, or had a cosseted existence. He may have been 'born in the purple' but his circumstances were not enviable, and a great deal of tragedy was crowded into his early years. Within months of his birth in 1921, his family was forced to flee their country, never to return. His father, blamed for failure in a military campaign he had never supported, was imprisoned by a revolutionary tribunal and sentenced to death by firing squad, to be reprieved only through the intervention of Britain's King George V. Instead, Prince Andrew was stripped of his military rank and Greek nationality, and banished in perpetuity. The family was rescued from an uncertain and hostile environment by a British cruiser, HMS *Calypso*, and the four-month-old prince was famously accommodated in a fruit crate adapted for the purpose by the crew.

Philip's father was to become a distant figure, later separating from his mother and having a somewhat rootless existence around Europe (he would die in Monte Carlo in 1944, aged sixty-two, at a time when his son could of course not reach this territory). Philip's mother, Princess Andrew of Greece, deaf throughout his lifetime, was to be diagnosed as a schizophrenic during his adolescence – although this would not prevent her from founding an order of nuns, and sheltering Jews and other refugees when back in Athens during the Second World War.

Lacking any permanent home, the boy grew up as a guest in the homes of relatives, and at a succession of schools. His first mentor – his guardian while he was in Britain – was George Mountbatten, Marquess of Milford Haven. A naval officer and a man of keen intelligence and winning charm, he had survived the Battle of Jutland – the greatest naval showdown of the Great War (as had Princess Elizabeth's father, King George). He provided a highly suitable example for Philip in his early years, but was to die of cancer in 1938.

Philip was a strong enough character to cope with this impermanent lifestyle. Self-contained, pragmatic and not given to introspection, 'I just had to get on with it,' he later said. 'You do. One does.' His life contained, of course, much that was agreeable. He was close to his sisters, all of whom would marry members of the German aristocracy, and in his teenage years he would enjoy idyllic summers at their homes. He also spent time in England, where he often stayed at Lynden Manor, the Milford Havens' Edwardian country house near Windsor.

Though his education would largely take place in Britain, and would give him the accent, the outlook, the love of sports and of the outdoors that would be typical of a public schoolboy, his education in fact began in France. Following their departure from Greece his family lived for a period of eight years in the Paris suburb of St Cloud, in a small house borrowed from his father's brother and sister-in-law. His first dose of education was at The Elms, a nearby international school that was run by an American couple. Pictures show Philip as a spirited boy, with an unruly thatch of fair hair, firing a bow in a game of Robin Hood and making hideous faces while chewing in a biscuit-eating contest – which he won. Here he acquired, for a time, an American drawl. He was by no means as wealthy as some of his contemporaries, and he developed an endearing habit of saving patiently for the things, such as a bicycle, that he needed.

The first British phase began in 1928, when Philip came to school at Cheam, an unusually old and blue-blooded prep school at which his Mountbatten cousin David, Earl of Medina, was already a pupil. He was a difficult boy for his schoolmates to quantify. He was a member of a royal family, but not one about which they knew anything. He did not talk about his connections with the House of Windsor, yet he would be invited to tea with Britain's own royals and might even stay at Kensington Palace. He had about him none of the physical trappings of royalty, and the only overt indication of his status was that he had no surname, being simply 'Philip of Greece'. He had the gifts that make any boy popular in such an environment. He was competent at work without being a genius or a swot, and he had an all-round ability at games that was impressive, playing for the school's first teams in rugby, soccer and cricket. He was noisy, given to pranks, and of a sociable nature, rather than shy or thoughtful. He thrived in the communal,

TOP: Prince Philip with the Junior Cricket Team (Philip is tossing the ball in the air), at Gordonstoun.

BOTTOM: Prince Philip, foreground, performs in a Robin Hood play at the MacJannet American School.

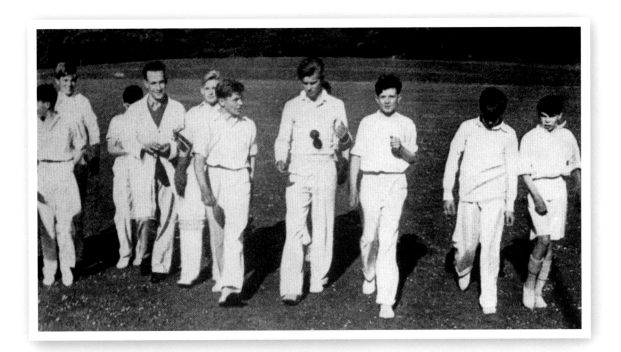

TOP: A twelve-year-old Prince Philip (2nd from left) takes part in an historical pageant at Gordonstoun.

BOTTOM: Prince Philip (centre left, kneeling) performs as King Melchior in a nativity play at his public school, Gordonstoun.

institutional atmosphere. His elders must have felt a sense of relief that despite the upheavals of his childhood and the uncertainty of his family circumstances he had settled so well into school in a country that was not his own.

From Cheam, however, he went back to the Continent to continue his education. The British upper class does not heavily patronize the sort of 'international schools' that exist in Switzerland and in other corners of Europe, for the United Kingdom has enough great schools of its own. Philip's time at Cheam had made him a highly suitable candidate for admission to a major public school.

However, Salem School on the shores of Lake Constance, Germany, was different. It was owned by his brother-in-law (whose father had founded it in 1918), and so he could go there without paying fees. Given the genteel poverty in which his parents lived, this was a decisive factor. Once again, Philip adapted extremely well. The school did not aspire to turn out scholars, and instead sought to develop character and leadership, not least through an outdoorish attention to exercise. This could have been tailor-made for the Prince, whose physical robustness was his most visible characteristic.

He might have remained in Germany for the whole of his secondary schooling, perhaps becoming in the process a very different personality, had events not intervened. He was sent to the school in 1934. The previous year, Hitler's National Socialist German Workers' Party had come to power in Germany. It had begun imposing its draconian agenda on the country, and the effects were gradually felt even in this tranquil corner of the Reich. Among other things, it made compulsory the use in public of the 'German greeting' – the straight-arm fascist salute – and this was adopted by Salem pupils. To Philip, trained in the less extreme ways of the English (and who, as a foreigner, was not obliged to make this gesture), the poker-faced fanaticism suggested by it was simply laughable – as was the fact that raising the right arm in this manner was associated in the minds of schoolchildren with 'asking to leave the room'.

Far more serious, however, was the fact that the school's guiding light, Dr Kurt Hahn, was a Jew. He could not expect to remain in the teaching profession, and took the decision to move to another country and continue his work there. He started again in a somewhat bleak setting near the north-east coast of Scotland. Philip was soon to join him; he had been returned by Fate to British soil.

The main house and outbuildings at Gordonstoun, the austere country residence of the Gordon-Cummings family near Elgin, were converted to accommodate a school that, unlike Salem, was for boys only. It bore some passing resemblance to a typical public school, though it had no traditions. It lacked the petty snobberies, the gradations of dress, the fetish for organized games and the fagging-and-flogging treatment of junior boys. None of this would have been easy to create or sustain in such a setting, even had Hahn wished to do so. Things tended to be comparatively easy-going at the school. The pupils wore comfortable, practical clothes. They played team games but in the knowledge that hill-climbing or sailing were just as important. They had a pioneering spirit such as people have when they know they are building for the future – literally, in many cases: one contribution to the facilities for which Philip was responsible was a pigsty. Senior boys had no traditional titles like Prefect or Monitor. The head boy was called the Guardian, and those who were entrusted by Hahn with lesser responsibilities were known quaintly as 'colour bearers' or simply 'helpers'. Elected by his contemporaries, Philip rose through this loose gradation to the top of the school. A report described him as 'a good school Guardian', though interestingly Hahn also observed that his leadership qualities were liable to be 'marred at times by impatience and intolerance'. Gordonstoun attracted the sons of a few idealistic intellectuals and a number of comfortably-off Scottish farmers and industrialists. It was not – until the time Philip sent his own sons there – seen as a place of any great social prestige.

Hahn had chosen the setting wisely. The moorland, the rugged

TOP: Prince Philip going out to bat for Gordonstoun, where he was captain, 1939.

FAR RIGHT: A rare picture of Prince Philip at Gordonstoun.

BOTTOM: Prince Philip is seen in the classroom at the MacJannet American School.

TOP: A general view of Gordonstoun.

BOTTOM: The Prince of Wales with his father Philip on his first day of his new school. To greet the new boy were the head boy Peter Paice, left, and the Senior Boy Dougal McKenzie with the Housemaster Robert Whitby, third from left, and the headmaster F.R.G. Chew, right.

coast and the unheated rooms enabled him to concentrate on the kind of character building in which he believed. His pupils were, by virtue of recent events, a cosmopolitan lot, but as the school began to attract the sons of moderately wealthy locals, its character became increasingly Scots. There were ample opportunities to learn leadership in the area, for Gordonstoun pupils took charge of the local fire brigade and coastguard units. They sailed in the nearby Moray Firth. Philip, who had never before had regular access to the sea, was delighted. He became a sea scout and a stalwart of the coastguard – he had considerable fun practising breeches-buoy drills with them. He was also a common sight in the harbour where he worked, mop-haired and clad in an old pullover or in dungarees, on the school boat alongside local fishermen on his half-holidays. They knew that this often scruffy young man, devoid of airs and graces, was a member of a royal family, but they referred to him as 'our Pheelup'. As if to prove his ordinariness, he sailed with some schoolfellows as far as Scandinavia and back, acting as ship's cook on the way.

His education perfectly suited his talents and his strengths. Though he was capable of original thought he was not an academic or an intellectual boy. He was later to say that, 'My favourite subject at school was avoiding unnecessary work,' and it is fair to surmise that he concentrated enough in areas that interested him without spending much time on learning for its own sake. Surprisingly, a subject he did not favour was history. Even if he had no inkling of his future role, it might have been assumed that any member of a royal house would have a head start in background knowledge, as well as an interest in important past events. He was, at any rate, to develop such an interest in all things historical at a later stage. For the moment, there was too much else to get on with.

His school, with its uncompromising regime of discomfort and exercise, was a most unusual environment for the upbringing of a royal, let alone one from southern Europe. Yet although he came to it by accident, it was just the place for a boy who loved outdoor activity, hard knocks and risk-taking. Philip was good at the customary schoolboy things. He was captain of the cricket and hockey XIs, appeared in the – albeit minor – role of Donalbain in a production of *Macbeth* (this led to the first, short, article about him in the British press), and showed enough qualities to be appointed Guardian one term – despite having had a headmaster's report that categorized him as 'wild and reckless'. Though this record is impressive, it is worth remembering that the competition for school honours was not great. When he began at Gordonstoun there were fewer than thirty pupils, and by the time he left there were only around a hundred. Inclusion in a team was not, as he himself would later tell an interviewer, a notable achievement; 'there were so few of us, anyone who could hold a bat was in.' Indeed the school did not even have its own playing fields at the time.

Perhaps more significant was the fact that he was allowed to go to sea without being accompanied by an adult. Such was his obvious leadership ability that he would have shone even in a much bigger school. His characteristics of confidence, humour and a desire to excel, as so often in a school, could be harnessed for the good of the community. In later years, someone rather sneeringly suggested to Queen Mary that his educational background had not fitted him for his future life. They had asked whether Gordonstoun had been useful or otherwise. 'Useful,' said the Queen, very firmly, and she was right. The school did not have in it a wide cross section of society – its pupils were from families wealthy enough to afford the fees – but it was a much more free and flexible environment than a traditional public school in the south would have been. The boys were not marked out from the host community by conspicuous or flamboyant uniforms, or by a distinctive accent, and nor were they isolated from their surroundings. As shown, they made a valuable contribution to the locality. The school was new and there was thus no sense of 'town–gown' animosity or resentment.

His final school report was to become famous. In it the

TOP LEFT: The Queen with Prince Andrew when he started at Gordonstoun.

TOP RIGHT: The Queen with a kilted Prince Edward (right) walks with Gordonstoun headmaster, Mr Michael Mavor, in the school grounds.

BOTTOM: The Queen and Prince Philip walk in the grounds of Gordonstoun with the school's Headmaster, Mr Michael Mavor (centre, left), and their youngest son, Prince Edward, the Head Boy and in his final term.

LEFT: Queen Elizabeth II
and Prince Philip at a State
dinner in Lagos, Nigeria,
1956.

headmaster offered yet more prescient observation: 'Prince Philip is a born leader, but it will need the exacting demands of a great service to do justice to himself. His best is outstanding; his second best is not good enough; Prince Philip will make his mark in any profession where he will have to prove himself in a full trial of strength.' (It was Dr Hahn, incidentally, who conceived the idea that became the Duke of Edinburgh's Award. Had it existed in the 1930s, the teenage Greek prince would have been an ideal, and archetypal, participant.)

When he was a schoolboy of sixteen one of Philip's sisters, Cecile, together with her husband the Grand Duke of Hesse and her two children, was killed in an air accident at Ostend while travelling to England. By the time he reached manhood, Philip had experienced as much sadness as many people see in a whole lifetime.

Much has been made of his uncle, Louis Mountbatten's, influence on him during adolescence, although Mountbatten was away at sea for much of Philip's youth. The older man was serious about his naval career, and pursued it with vigour. He combined this, however, with the image of a playboy. He was married to the fabulously wealthy Edwina Ashley, and her money enabled him to live in considerable style with a country house, Broadlands, in Hampshire (at which both Philip and his eldest son would stay during their honeymoons) and a beautiful penthouse in Mayfair. A friend of Noël Coward, who would later play him in the film *In Which We Serve*, Mountbatten was one of the most glamorous figures in inter-war British society. Though the physical resemblance between Mountbatten and the grown-up Prince Philip was not striking, they had the same voice, the same way of speaking, the same manner, the same urbanity. There can be little doubt the Philip admired Mountbatten's easy charm, sporting prowess and professional ability, for any boy would have done so.

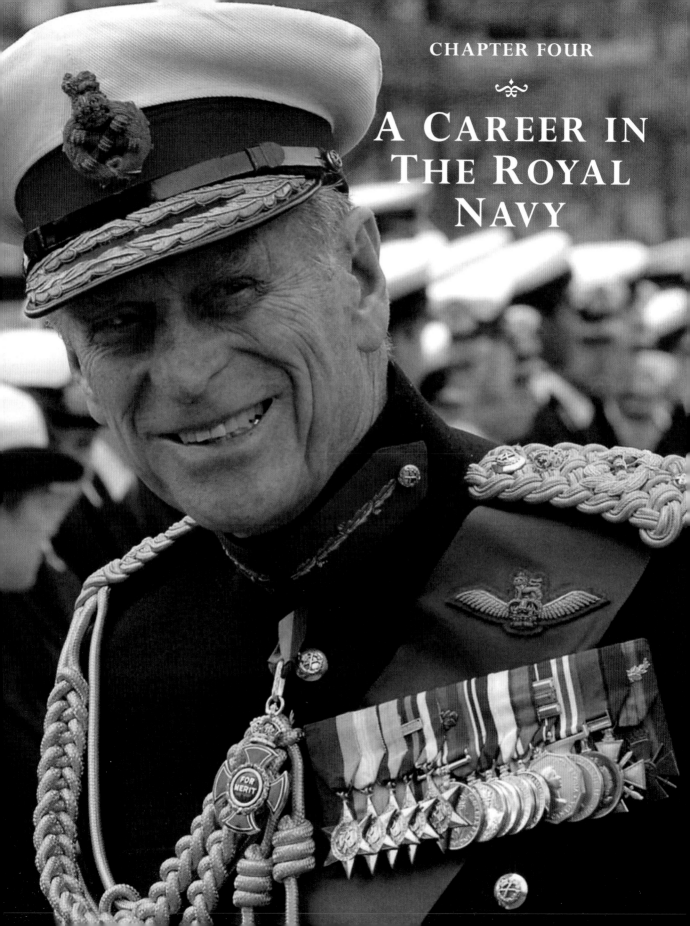

A Career in The Royal Navy

PREVIOUS SPREAD: Philip
meets young sailors
after attending a church
service to mark the 25th
anniversary of the Falkland
Islands' liberation at the
Falkland Islands Memorial
Chapel at Pangbourne
College in Berkshire.

LEFT: Philip as
Commander of the Frigate
HMS *Magpie* in 1951.

Prince Philip did not aspire to attend university, though he was undoubtedly intelligent enough to do so, and in those days his name would have been enough to open the doors of some socially conscious Oxbridge college. He was bent on a career in the Services, and was later to say that he had wanted to join the RAF. He would have sought to be a fighter pilot, and it has been pointed out that, had he done so, he would have been just in time to take part in the Battle of Britain — with the result that he might well not have survived. His uncle, Mountbatten, persuaded him that the Navy was more acceptable for someone of his status and he had, after all, developed a genuine love of boats and sailing and an ability in handling craft. In other words, he was very fortunate in that, from adolescence, he decided on a profession for which his leanings and abilities made him ideally suited. (He was later to make light of what must have been a sense of vocation. 'I had to think of something to do for a living,' he said.)

A career in the Navy requires genuine practical ability and intelligence, and Philip had these qualities in abundance. Another quality — technical knowledge — can be taught, but here too he had an interest in 'how things work' that carried him a long way, and enabled him to cram for examinations without difficulty. From Dartmouth it would simply be a case of applying himself and of passing through the necessary stages, to a commission as an officer and then promotion through the ranks. Though he joined on the understanding that he would transfer to the Royal Hellenic Navy if circumstances permitted, he will also have thought in terms of regular British service.

His uncle was to become Admiral of the Fleet as well as — during the coming war — Supreme Commander South East Asia. His great-uncle, Prince Louis of Battenberg, had been First Sea Lord. Philip's own hopes and ambitions could have fixed on some similar professional horizon. He had the aptitude, he had the family background with the Service, he had the intelligence and — thanks to long hours of sailing in the Moray Firth — he had a developed a lasting love of the sea. His practical confidence was ideally suited for a career that would involve quick decisions, whether on how to manoeuvre a ship into harbour or when to open fire on an oncoming enemy vessel.

Approaching his eighteenth birthday, Philip entered Dartmouth in May 1939 for a six-month training course. He joined late, after the rest of his entry, so his subsequent success means he had overtaken other cadets who had had more time to learn. He was beginning in the Navy at a time when war was very likely to break out, and of course he will have been aware, not least through the network of his relations and his highly placed uncle, of how grave the international situation was. It was a most challenging and dangerous time to be embarking on a career in the Service, but from a professional viewpoint a most rewarding one. There would be opportunities for enterprise, heroism, promotion and command that peacetime could not readily offer.

By virtue of residence and education, Philip had grown up British, in the sense that his experiences, accent, friendships and mind-set were those of the British upper class. He was, however, still Greek. If the political climate were to change in his home country he might, at short notice, have to return there and take up a ceremonial role. If not, he would need to become a naturalized British citizen in order to make a long-term career in the Royal Navy. His future was therefore not as entirely cut-and-dried as it may have seemed. Britain was expecting war, but Greece was neutral. Would he – could he – serve in a conflict on behalf of a country that was not officially his own?

As a young man entering the world, what were Philip's marriage prospects? The era of arranged marriages between dynasties was over. The Great War had toppled many thrones, but choosing a partner from a deposed or exiled royal house would have been entirely acceptable. He could, as his sisters were to do, have married some member of the numerous German aristocracy. Had this happened, and had he been able to live in the National Socialist state without compromising his integrity, this anglophile young man would have faced a painful

TOP: Lieutenant Philip Mountbatten (fifth from left, front row), with Course No. 17 at the Royal Naval Petty Officers School, Kingsmoor, Corsham, Wiltshire.

BOTTOM: Prince Philip smiles during a naval visit to Melbourne, Australia, 1945.

TOP: Princess Elizabeth
dancing with her fiancé
at the Assembly Rooms,
Edinburgh, when a ball was
held to welcome the royal
family to Scotland.

BOTTOM: King George
VI and Queen Elizabeth
arrive at Romsey Abbey
in the New Forest with
bridesmaids Princesses
Elizabeth and Margaret,
for the wedding of Patricia
Mountbatten (the daughter
of Viscount Mountbatten)
and Lord Brabourne. Philip
can be seen, right.

dilemma once war broke out. Given such ambivalence, and Hitler's nervous animosity toward princes ('The Third Reich needs no royal defenders,' he said, and made sure that they were kept out of positions of influence), Philip would almost certainly have been spied upon and found himself in trouble with the authorities. His sisters, married to men who were close to the Party, were themselves not in danger, but their influence might not have been able to save him.

His connections with Britain's ruling house, his background of living and working in the country and his age suitability with regard to the two daughters of King George VI made the possibility of a marriage to one of them by no means an idle notion. The princesses would be likely to marry compatriots, not only because of a lack of potential foreign suitors but because their father, who doted upon them both, would have been reluctant to see them go to live abroad. It was therefore possible that they would wed senior members of the British aristocracy. They would, however, be allowed to marry for love. The King's own marriage had been spectacularly happy and he would have wanted nothing less for the girls. There were very few young dukes whose affections were not already committed, or who had the freedom (from running their own estates) or the temperament to be a successful consort. Finding a husband for Princess Elizabeth was going to be a difficult task. He must be a man of suitable status, as well as someone acceptable to the British people and those of the Commonwealth and Empire. Whoever it was, he would need to be able to play a supporting role to his wife, yet have his own personality.

Philip fitted the bill in almost every way. He had in a sense been bred to the life since adolescence through the influence of his uncle. Such grooming of a consort was not without precedent. Victoria's husband, Prince Albert, had been assiduously trained by his own uncle, Leopold of Belgium, from early manhood for this same role – and of course had carried it out with great success.

The account of the meeting between Philip and Elizabeth was first revealed in a book by the princess's governess, Marion Crawford. In the summer of 1939, Elizabeth accompanied her sister and her parents on a visit to the Naval College aboard the royal yacht. There had been an outbreak of mumps, and this meant that the girls had to be kept apart from the cadets. Mountbatten was there, by now established as mentor to Prince Philip, and he arranged for the young man to be assigned to the royal party as the Captain's 'doggie' – a general factotum to the commanding officer. This meant that he was highly visible throughout the day. He was also told to look after the girls while their parents planted a tree and toured the college, and it is unlikely that the prospect of babysitting two young girls – then aged thirteen and eight – much appealed to him. The three young people played with a model railway and then went outside to a tennis court, where Philip impressed his future wife with his ability to jump over the net. The whole party later had tea. The yacht remained at anchor overnight and Philip was one of those invited aboard to dinner that evening, but he did not see Elizabeth, who had already been sent to bed.

By the next afternoon, when Philip again came aboard to tea, the Princess seemed to hang on his every word. Some time later, when the vessel departed, cadets followed it out of Dartmouth Harbour in small boats. As the distance increased, more and more of them faded from sight, and only a single one continued to follow. It was Philip. Though he was later to earn a reputation for sound common sense, this was a very foolish thing to do. The King had him ordered back for fear that he would go too far out and be unable to return, obliging the yacht to hoist him aboard. According to Miss Crawford, her younger charge, Princess Margaret, looked at Elizabeth and noticed that she was crying.

This is a pleasant story, though one that both the Queen and her husband may well be tired of hearing. Dartmouth was not actually their first meeting – they had had at least one previous encounter, at the coronation of Elizabeth's father in 1937 – but neither of them could remember anything of previous occasions, and the day they spent at the Naval College therefore deserves to be seen as the start of their friendship. They began to write to each other after that, and though

TOP: Lieutenant Philip Mountbatten (third from the left of those standing) taking part in a game of skittles with brother officers at the 'local', the Methuen Arms, Corsham, Wiltshire.

BOTTOM: The newly designed coat-of-arms for Lieutenant Philip Mountbatten, RN. The design bears the arms of Princess Alice, Lieutenant Mountbatten's grandmother, over all in the first quarter, on the arms of Denmark and Greece. The supporters are Hercules, representing Greece, and the Lion of England gorged with a naval crown. The crest has five ostrich feathers derived from the Carisbrooke and Mountbatten arms.

GOD IS MY HELP

this correspondence was irregular at first, their letters became more frequent. It is unlikely that Philip thought of the shy schoolgirl as a serious companion at first, but the notion clearly took hold. When later as a young officer he arrived to join HMS *Ramillies* for service in the Mediterranean the vessel's captain, Vice-Admiral Harold Baillie-Grohman, interviewed him. Asked about his thoughts on the future, Philip candidly replied that: 'My Uncle Dickie has plans for me. He thinks I could marry Princess Elizabeth.' The Admiral was rather taken aback. 'Are you really fond of her?' he asked. 'Oh yes, very,' was the reply, 'I write to her every week.'

And apparently he did. As so often happens with young women, Elizabeth seemed to blossom from a child into an adult virtually overnight, her hairstyle, her clothing and her manner all becoming suddenly more mature. Philip and the Princess found they shared a sense of humour and liked the same things. They went dancing and to the theatre, and they enjoyed musicals more than straight plays – they were to see *Oklahoma!* more than once, and Elizabeth learned some songs from the show. They of course had their background in common, having grown up surrounded by some of the same relations, and in an atmosphere of protocol and precedence. Elizabeth had always had the companionship of her younger sister, but in Philip, who was five years her senior, she had a man of seemingly limitless energy, wit and enterprise. His company must have been an education, bringing a sense of adventure to a young woman whose life had previously been hedged around by formality, protection and protocol.

Philip was a very easy young man to fall in love with. He was spectacularly attractive at all ages from childhood onwards. As an eighteen-year-old naval cadet he was the epitome of vigorous, glamorous young manhood. Princess Elizabeth had never met a boy with such striking looks, such noisy confidence or such brash lack of deference. His temperament and personality bore no resemblance to those of her father, and most young men who met her were reduced by her position to a shyness that matched her own. With Philip it was an attraction of opposites; he simply had qualities that she lacked, though she herself was to demonstrate very considerable abilities of her own. His love of showing off deeply impressed her and there is absolutely no evidence that she was ever to think of any other man as a potential husband. Her parents came to like him too, so that he received invitations to Buckingham Palace or Windsor when he was on leave.

Philip passed out of the college at the head of his year. As well as being Cadet Captain he was awarded the King's Dirk, which is the nautical equivalent of the Sword of Honour awarded to the best cadets at Sandhurst and Cranwell. If this were not glory enough, he also received the Eardley-Howard-Crockett Prize for being best cadet – a book token which he spent on appropriate reading matter: *The Defence of Britain* by the great military theorist Basil Liddell Hart. By that time the expected war had been declared, even if fighting in Europe had not yet actually begun.

At the start of the following year he was posted to sea duty aboard a battleship and then served in two cruisers, ferrying troops across the Indian Ocean. As a very minor historical footnote it is perhaps worth mentioning that a relic of his visit to this region can still be seen. The Galle Face Hotel in Colombo, Sri Lanka, has its own museum, and one of the exhibits is a small motor car. A sign on this explains that it was the first automobile owned by Prince Philip, and had been bought during a shore leave on the island. Then in 1941 Philip was in the Mediterranean, a more suitable theatre for a Greek prince, and here he was to see action. He took part in the battle off Cape Matapan that was to eliminate any threat from the Italian surface fleet for the rest of the war. He was not involved in firing guns but in controlling searchlights – an important aspect of an engagement that was fought at night.

Curiously, although he enjoyed displaying his physical abilities – swimming, rowing, sailing, driving (at which he was impatient, and once ended up in a ditch), he was circumspect about actual heroism. While we cannot know the contents of his wartime letters

LEFT: Philip at the helm
of Owen Aisher's yacht
Yeeman, under sail during
the Cowes Regatta.

to Elizabeth, it is clear from his communications with others that he
described actions in which he had taken part with a good deal of laconic
self-effacement. He was in real and sustained danger on many occasions,
yet his descriptions play this down and make light of it.

His log, written in 1941 – a personal record that all junior naval
officers were obliged to keep – refers to attacks on HMS *Valiant* by
enemy aircraft, which, after strafing the *Illustrious*, 'concentrated on us
and five bombs dropped fairly close and a number of splinters fell on the
ship', though these caused no casualties. He goes on to say that fourteen
dive-bombers returned to the attack and that 'one Dornier came
straight for us from the port beam and dropped 12 bombs when he
was almost overhead'. Exciting stuff. His commanding officer, Admiral
Sir Andrew Cunningham, wrote of him in his report that 'Thanks to
his alertness and appreciation of the situation, we were able to sink in
five minutes two eight-inch gun cruisers.' Mention in despatches is a
considerable honour, though less of one than receiving a medal. Philip
may not have been decorated by the British government for his part in
the action, but he did receive a form of recognition from the country
of his birth: he was given the Greek War Cross. It was one of three
decorations with which its government would reward him.

Another thing he achieved, after transferring to another part of
the world, was a boiler trimmer's certificate for acting as a stoker.
Sailing with other midshipmen aboard a superannuated 'rust-bucket' to
Canada to pick up and transport troops to Europe, the vessel lost all its
Chinese stokers, who all quit at Puerto Rico. From there to the United
States, Philip and his colleagues had to shovel the coal that powered the
engines. It must have been dirty and exhausting, but it gave him one
more strand of wartime experience.

He was soon promoted, through a combination of excellent
results in training courses and valuable shipboard experience. He went
from midshipman to sub-lieutenant, lieutenant and first lieutenant in
the space of two years, becoming, at twenty-one, one of the Navy's
youngest holders of that rank. By that time he had been assigned to

somewhat routine, if dangerous, convoy escort and anti-submarine duties up and down the east coast of Britain.

Returning to the Mediterranean, Philip's ship was involved in the landings on Sicily and on the Italian mainland. After this he was posted to an entirely different war on the other side of the world. As first lieutenant aboard the newly commissioned HMS *Whelp*, he went to the Pacific to fight the Japanese where his flotilla was responsible for firing on oilfields in the Dutch East Indies to deny them to the enemy, and saw action off the Burmese coast. This was in 1944. The war in Europe was thought to be in its final stage, though increasingly desperate German resistance would prolong the conflict until halfway through the following year. Japan too was clearly on the back foot, retreating from one conquered territory after another in the face of American, British and Australian onslaughts. The Japanese home islands, however, had yet to be invaded, and this operation was likely to be very costly in Allied lives. A million casualties were expected, and it was also envisaged as a long operation, lasting perhaps until 1948. Philip might therefore have expected this phase of the war to be the most significant, as well as the most dangerous.

In the event, the atomic bombs dropped in August 1945 brought the surrender of the Japanese nation and its forces without the need for invasion. *Whelp* was sent to Tokyo Bay and she was moored nearby when the capitulation was signed on the deck of the battleship USS *Missouri*. Philip's presence at this important, yet seemingly now remote, moment in history enhances the sense of timelessness that seems to attach to him. His varied war service, which took him from the coast of North America to the shores of Australia, is the reason he was awarded so many campaign medals. The British are seen by other countries as parsimonious when it comes to giving medals, and sailors in any case win fewer of these than soldiers. Philip, however, qualified for several of the campaign stars given for war service: Atlantic, Africa, Italy and Burma (with the clasp for service in the Pacific). This would enhance his sense of solidarity with veterans in the years ahead, and

LEFT: Princess Elizabeth smiling happily as, with Philip, she enjoys the sunshine of Malta in the garden of the Villa Guardamangia. Prince Philip was serving in Malta as First Lieutenant on board C Class Destroyer and Flotilla Leader, HMS *Chequers*.

increase their respect for him. In 1995, when there were celebrations in the Mall to mark the fiftieth anniversary of VJ Day — the victory over Japan — Prince Philip slipped away from the dais from which he and the Queen had been watching the passing parade. He reappeared shortly afterwards, marching in the contingent of Burma Star veterans and wearing a beret adorned with their cap-badge, a fitting and very popular gesture.

Naturally, the friendship between Philip and Elizabeth pleased several of the adults who were concerned with their futures. Lord Mountbatten was delighted that his protégé was genuinely fond of the Princess and that this feeling was reciprocated, though he himself had urged his nephew on with such enthusiasm that the younger man had written to his uncle: 'Please, I beg of you, not too much advice in an affair of the heart or I shall be forced to do the wooing by proxy.' Queen Mary liked him, and saw in him a valuable recruit for the family, though his manner with the public — either relaxed and jocular or sometimes testy — was a world away from her own. He fitted the times, while she did not.

Interestingly, another influential section of opinion that had a view on Philip's suitability was the public. Whatever the glamour of his appearance, never mind that he looked like an Anglo-Saxon and spoke like the product of an English public school, however distinguished the war record he had accumulated in the service of their country, the people over whom the Princess would one day rule did not take to him. He was perceived as a foreigner throughout the courtship, and this was a significant black mark against him. In fact, a survey carried out by the *Sunday Pictorial* found that forty per cent of readers were against the notion of his marrying Elizabeth. Greece was a politically volatile and unstable country, then in the grip of a painful civil war in which British troops were in danger of becoming seriously involved. A link with this nation might cause that deeper involvement to happen. At best it might prove an international embarrassment. The Labour government was uneasy. The Princess, however, had made up her mind.

For the moment, Philip had to hang fire. Greece had recently allowed its royal family to return, and there was a notion that if a member of the ruling house chose to abandon the country and become a citizen elsewhere it might prove a very serious drawback to the restored monarchy.

Now a regular officer in the peacetime Navy, Philip was sent to Wiltshire to join the staff of a school for instructing petty officers, HMS *Royal Arthur*. It is, in the Services, always a compliment to the abilities of an individual that he is made an instructor. It implies not only that he thinks clearly and communicates well but is fit to serve as an example to others. Philip became generally popular, and though he chafed at the work – endlessly repeating formulae – he was a genuinely inspiring speaker with a gift for explaining and he was respected by the men he taught. He also devoted himself to cricket (Sir Donald Bradman, who would later see him play, was to describe him as a 'very useful' bowler) and soccer (he played in goal, the position he had made his own on the XI at Cheam), and would make famous the skittle alley in the nearby pub at Corsham, the Methuen Arms, where he played this game against the locals with customary intensity.

His posting a matter of miles west of London also meant that he was within driving distance of the Palace and of Windsor. The relationship was now public property. The Princess was occasionally heckled during official visits with shouts of 'Where's Philip?' He was long accustomed to open gossip among ships' crews, and speculation among society hostesses and journalists. Why else, after all, would this foreign prince still be hanging about in Britain? The tide of rumour continued to swell, yet there was no official announcement. Months passed without word.

CHAPTER FIVE

✥

PHILIP AND ELIZABETH

In the autumn of 1946 Philip was invited to Balmoral. Even without his connection to the Princess, this personable young man was a welcome guest of the King and Queen. He fitted in easily with their tastes and pursuits, and his enjoyment of the rugged charms of Balmoral will have confirmed his suitability as a member of the family.

At some point during the weeks he spent there he proposed to Elizabeth and she accepted. Her father's permission was naturally asked and, though he had had some personal doubts, he too agreed. Not only did he like his future son-in-law, he could also see in him the promise of a new era for the monarchy. The Royal Family had been dominated by women – his mother, his wife, his daughters. It would help provide balance to have on board a charismatic, handsome and overtly masculine new member, and one who had shared – creditably, even heroically – in the common ordeal of war service. Perhaps, too, in the post-war atmosphere of egalitarianism, it would be useful to have a son-in-law who had not grown up in luxury and had lived modestly.

While the King and Queen were fond of him – and while history has resoundingly proved them right in their assessment – courtiers regarded him with more circumspection. The fellow simply lacked polish. Along with his self-confidence, he was seen as noisy and bumptious. He lacked deference, seemed unwilling to be taught, and was quite capable of hurting feelings or saying the wrong thing. Anyone taking on the role of consort would need considerable diplomatic skill, as well as a good deal of patience with formality and ceremony. Philip had not demonstrated these things. The schoolboy who had had little interest in history did not show a proper respect for the dignity of an historical institution or those who upheld it (it is easy to imagine how fustian and humourless these officials must have seemed, in their turn, to him). One observer, Sir Harold Nicholson, commented gloomily that he found the young man 'Rough, uneducated and [liable to be] unfaithful.'

This latter point was important. Philip was well aware of his handsome appearance, and so was London society. He had close, if innocent, friendships with several attractive young women. Some of them were relations, some old family friends, and some were simply acquaintances from London cocktail parties. These included his cousin Alexandra (who became Queen of Yugoslavia) and a Canadian heiress of striking beauty called Osla Benning, whom he had met during the war. Sometimes feelings had gone deeper, and Elizabeth was not his first love. His inclination to flirt, and towards friendships that would perhaps be inappropriate for a high-profile married man, will have caused some official disquiet. Whatever the truth of a situation, rumour and innuendo could be damaging. Both the King and the Prime Minister, Winston Churchill, had frank talks with the young man and impressed on him the importance of impeccable behaviour. He would in future be under continuous public scrutiny, though no one – in those years before modern media had fully developed – could have foreseen how intrusive and relentless this was to be.

While huffy remarks about his flirtatious nature may seem like the mere blowing off of steam by the Palace's old guard, it is worth remembering that these men had very considerable influence while King George was alive, and that this very largely continued after his death. Elizabeth's accession was so swift that without the reassuring continuity brought by their presence the early days of her reign would have been very difficult. She also wanted to preserve as much as possible of the methods and practices her father had followed.

Courtiers who disapproved of Philip had no lack of opportunities to put him in his place. Though he was a self-contained individual, though his future wife was overwhelmingly fond of him and though his background had imbued him with considerable toughness, he was not given an easy ride by the Palace or by the public. For a man who has always been more sensitive than outward appearances suggest, it must have been a very considerable ordeal. That he was willing to leave a largely carefree existence as a successful naval officer for

RIGHT: Philip wearing jeans and a checked shirt, in a square dance in Ottawa.

LEFT: Philip at Northolt
Aerodrome as he
bids farewell to the
Viscount and Viscountess
Mountbatten who were
travelling to India.

the frustrations of life at court, and to plan to abandon for good the career he had chosen when his wife's destiny caught up with her, is surely all the evidence that observers could need of the strength of his feelings for her.

There were twin obstacles to be cleared away if Philip was to become legally able to marry the Princess: he must join the Church of England, and he must attain British citizenship. The former was an easy matter. He was sent to the Archbishop of Canterbury at Lambeth Palace, and the necessary formalities for removing him from the Greek Orthodox Church and installing him in the Anglican one were carried out as swiftly as a dental appointment.

Naturalization was something he had considered for years. As a member of the Royal Navy, and with a career in this service now likely to be his future, a change of citizenship would be necessary. This was a significant step for the young man to take, however, for in doing so he must renounce any claim to the throne of Greece. The country had not been his home, and members of his family had little reason to regard it with affection. Nevertheless his status as a Prince of Greece – his badge of membership of European royalty – was not something to be lightly cast aside. It was obvious, however, that Britain could offer him a future, and – if the relationship with Princess Elizabeth continued to flourish – a useful role in the life of the nation. With so much of his family and his own past already connected to Britain, naturalization must have seemed preferable to an uncertain connection with an unstable country. He completed this process, after lengthy bureaucratic delays, in February 1947. The news that he was now a British citizen led to an outburst of speculation in the press that an announcement of his engagement was imminent.

She was twenty, he was twenty-five. Her father did not want the news to be released until after her twenty-first birthday, which would fall in April 1947. By that time she would be in South Africa with her parents and sister, undertaking a major tour of the Dominion. This was an event of sufficient importance to eclipse an announcement of the engagement, though the South Africans would have been delighted had they known. In order that the public would not jump to conclusions, Philip was forbidden either to see the party off on their journey or to be present when they returned. He had already, however, been photographed with the Royal Family at the wedding of Mountbatten's daughter Patricia, and despite the innocent fact that both he and the Windsors were relatives of the bride, speculation had intensified.

At last, on 10 July 1947, the engagement was made public. The announcement read:

> It is with the greatest pleasure that the King and Queen announce the betrothal of their dearly beloved daughter The Princess Elizabeth to Lieutenant Philip Mountbatten, RN … to which union the King has gladly given his consent.

Shortly afterwards they appeared as a couple at a Buckingham Palace garden party. Philip had renounced his Greek citizenship and with it the privilege of being known only by his Christian name. Needing a surname for the first time in his life, both he and the appropriate experts cast around for one. 'Sonderburg-Glücksberg' had a Germanic ring that was deeply inappropriate in 1947. 'Oldcastle', the literal translation of Oldenburg, was clumsy, and sounded contrived. Given the influence of his mother's family in his life it was not surprising – and a nice compliment – that he adopted her name and became Philip Mountbatten, though it does not sound as if he was especially enthusiastic; 'I couldn't think of a reasonable alternative,' he was later to say. It is likely that he resented the notion that his rise in the Navy might be linked to a famous relative whose name he now bore. Nevertheless, it much pleased his uncle.

He was referred to thereafter in the press as 'Lieutenant Mountbatten' and sometimes even as 'Mister Mountbatten'– despite the supposedly egalitarian spirit of the times, there were snobbish jokes

RIGHT: Princess Elizabeth and Philip pose for their first engagement pictures at Buckingham Palace.

about the groom's comparative poverty. It was common knowledge that a naval officer of his rank earned only £11 a week, and that he had no private resources (he had to save up to buy his fiancée an engagement ring). It was asserted that his wardrobe consisted only of his naval officer's uniform, which was not a great exaggeration, and that he spent his leave staying with one relative or another. This was certainly true, as he told a friend: 'Do you know I've never really had a home. Since I was eight I've always been away at school or in the Navy.'

While he might have been short of possessions, he was about to gain further titles. The day before his wedding, the King created him Baron Greenwich (highly appropriate for a naval officer), Earl of Merioneth and Duke of Edinburgh. He was also installed as a Knight of the Garter. From being a prince – albeit a rather Ruritanian one in the eyes of some – he had become merely a lieutenant before taking several steps up the ranks of the British aristocracy at once, attaining an earldom and a dukedom at the same time. 'It is rather a lot,' said the King, 'but Philip is mature enough to deal with it.'

One thing he lost, in exchange for this new status, was the habit of smoking. Smoking was, of course, much more common then than now, and would have been second nature to thousands of young men who had whiled away cold nights standing watch aboard ship. Princess Elizabeth, whose father was a heavy and lifelong consumer of cigarettes, disliked smoking and could not have been comfortably married to someone who indulged in it. Philip, with characteristic lack of fuss, did not wean himself gently off the habit but simply stopped – a rather charming present to his fiancée.

A huge amount of public interest focused on the wedding, driven by a flood of pictures and articles in the press. The two major participants were young, attractive and charismatic – as glamorous as film stars but with the added appeal of tradition and patriotism – and readers could not get enough information about them. This was also an international party that would focus attention on Britain and on the things that the British do best. Enthusiasts followed the rumours about

Elizabeth's dress, which was to be made by Norman Hartnell and for which she received a hundred extra clothing coupons. They discovered that she had been able to choose the design from twelve that had been shown her, though naturally the full glory of Hartnell's pearl-white, pearl-studded creation – which had a train fifteen feet long – would not be revealed until the day itself. The public also knew about her ring (Welsh gold) and about the presents that were piling up from all over the world (the total would be 1,347). These would be put on display and would bring many thousands to queue outside St James's Palace for the chance to be dazzled by the sheer opulence of it all.

RIGHT: Princess Elizabeth and Philip on their wedding day.

Most significantly, the event would be broadcast, and there would be cameras positioned outside the west door of the Abbey. The service would be heard by an audience of millions, even if it could not be seen. This represented a milestone in the monarchy's relations with its people – a feeling that the nation, the Commonwealth and the wider world could and should be included in the events inside the church. Within a few years the next great state occasion – the Coronation – would also be shared with the public and this time the cameras would be inside.

The marriage took place at Westminster Abbey on 20 November 1947. It was a dreary time of year and the capital, still in those days shrouded in black chimney smoke, looked as grim as the mood of a nation still suffering from rationing and shortages. The wedding was, in fact, the first glimpse of colour and elegance on the city's streets since the King's coronation a decade previously. It was also the first time since the war that the carriages and the troops' ceremonial uniforms had been seen, and this splendour had been approved by the left-wing Labour government of the time. The spectacle was magnificent, and most of those who crowded the pavements to watch did not realize how much scrounging, borrowing and adapting had had to go on in order to equip the soldiers.

On the day itself Philip arrived from Kensington Palace where he had been staying, doubtless still feeling the effects of a lively stag party

held at the Dorchester the night before. The bride came by coach, and was escorted up the aisle by the King to a wedding march that, like all the music that day, she had chosen herself. Her father later wrote to her that: 'You were so calm and composed during the service & said your words with such conviction that I knew everything was all right.'

Two thousand people, invited by the bride and groom and including a host of friends, colleagues, employees, former teachers and even chance acquaintances, filled the Abbey – including members of the skittles team from the Methuen Arms, the village pub at Corsham at which Philip had played in matches between the Navy and the locals. When the service ended, the couple returned to the Palace for a wedding breakfast of game from the Sandringham Estate. Rationing was still in force for a number of foods and ration cards had had to be obtained from the government for many of the foreign guests who were attending. Once the banquet was over, Elizabeth and Philip went in an open carriage (it was November, but they wanted the crowds to be able to see them) to Waterloo Station, there to travel to Broadlands, the home of Lord Mountbatten, where their honeymoon would begin. It would continue amid the chill and rough-hewn landscape of Balmoral.

When Philip married, he knew that royal duties would take some of his time, and that his wife would have many more of them than he would. Nevertheless, Elizabeth's father was only fifty-two at the time of the marriage, and it was expected that he would live into the 1960s. Philip therefore approached with seriousness the courses he undertook to gain promotion. There is no question that he had the ability and the ambition to have gone to the top of his profession.

He had a highly developed competitive edge, which was combined with a love of fitness. He kept his weight down by running with multiple sweaters on and he played cricket often, with whoever was to hand. He assembled assorted staff from the couple's weekend home in Buckinghamshire into a team, and practised the game relentlessly in odd moments, taking some of these staff members away from their duties to bowl or bat.

Philip was quickly steered towards public duties and activities that suited his youth and dynamism. He became President of the Marylebone Cricket Club. He joined the Jockey Club (despite a lukewarm interest in racing) and the Royal Yacht Squadron. He attended cup finals and presented trophies to the winners of rugby and boxing matches. He became a frequent visitor to youth clubs.

Most significantly, he was asked to become President of the National Playing Fields Association (NPFA), an organization dedicated to establishing as many playing fields as possible in order to create healthy future generations through access to fresh air and sports. Lord Mountbatten had held the post, and had been proving effective in it. The King, however, realized that it would be a useful means both of putting Philip in touch with the nation's youth and of getting him involved with communities all over the country. Mountbatten was persuaded into passing on the position. Philip was genuinely keen on this project, and went about his task as its representative with characteristic drive – he was to draw public attention to the need for more such facilities, to oversee the raising of funds, and to put pressure on local authorities and landowners to make spaces available. With Philip it became a passion. He even took part in a film – co-starring with Bob Hope, of all people – to help heighten awareness and fill the coffers. He played himself, genially helping a number of disadvantaged boys who had written to tell him they had nowhere to play.

Philip also began what would become a lifetime's habit of following his wife as she carried out official duties. He was still, of course, a serving naval officer and was having to combine this role with an increasing number of public duties. Fortunately he was posted to the Admiralty in Whitehall. It is a ten-minute walk from Buckingham Palace and he went there each day … on foot. On his return through the London twilight, the Princess could sometimes be glimpsed at a window of the Palace, looking out for him. Following this tour of duty

TOP: The crowd of people who gathered outside Buckingham Palace following a statement that an announcement will be made by the King on Princess Elizabeth's engagement.

BOTTOM: From left to right, King George VI, Princess Margaret, Lady Mary Cambridge, the bride and bridegroom, Queen Elizabeth and Queen Mary.

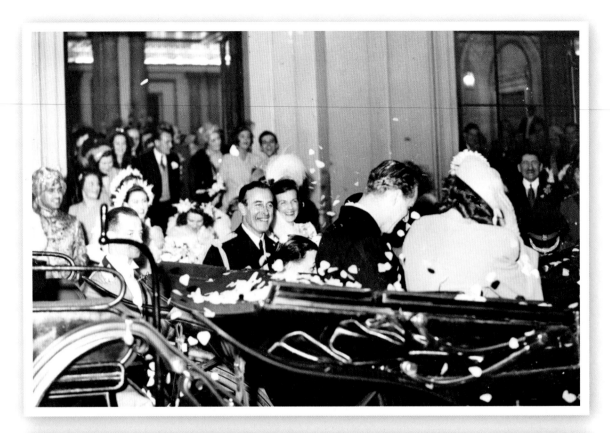

TOP: Princess Elizabeth
and Philip in a carriage
procession to Waterloo
Station for their train to
Winchester for the start of
their honeymoon.

BOTTOM: King Michael
I of Romania, right, with
the Queen Mother of
Romania, Elena, left, and
the Duchess of Aosta,
centre, are seen leaving
their London hotel, on
17 November 1947, to
attend the dance given by
King George VI and Queen
Elizabeth at Buckingham
Palace for friends of
Princess Elizabeth
and Lieutenant Philip
Mountbatten.

he was also sent to the naval staff college to undertake a course, but as this was in Greenwich he was still within reach.

One thing the Palace soon took for granted was his ferocious energy. He did not turn down engagements (that necessity would come later, as his diary simply became too full). He would always oblige if he could, and in the process he became the most active member the family had ever had. He could show interest even in the most esoteric organizations or events, and he was willing to 'say a few words' on virtually any occasion, often without the need for any notes. Philip gained a reputation for outspokenness because he had to make an increasing number of speeches, and he insisted on two things. One was that he would write them himself. It is perfectly acceptable – and often necessary for reasons of protocol – that royalty read speeches that are written by the Home Office, the Foreign Office or, as is the case at the state opening of Parliament, the government. Words are crafted to fit a host of diplomatic or political imperatives, to avoid partisan sentiments, personal opinions, unintentional offence to people or places, parties or countries. They are also written by others because royalty does not have the time to compose them, or may not have sufficient knowledge of the subject. Philip's speeches had to be cleared with the Palace, but he could – and felt he should – make them more lively and thought-provoking than the bland utterances that were expected from the Royal Family. His wife, once she became Queen, simply could not have had the luxury of expressing her own thoughts. Philip, in other words, believed he could be frank because he was neither on the throne nor in the line of succession. He had the freedom to say what the other members of the family could not.

And this was the second point. He wanted his speeches actually to say something. If he felt that his audience needed to be shaken out of complacent torpor, or reminded of their obligations to some good cause, he would not spare their feelings. This directness suited his no-nonsense nature and gained him respect. The fact that he also possessed an ebullient, sometimes mocking, sense of humour added to the impact. Within a short time he was regarded as one of the country's most popular after-dinner speakers, and his words were followed with interest by press and public.

He was the first Royal to put humour into his speeches. Previously this had simply not been done. Monarchs since Queen Victoria had been conditioned not to make jokes or ever to be seen laughing in public. Even the jovial Edward VII did not do these things. George V hid a poker face behind a full beard, and told his sons that they must never look amused or seek to be entertaining. Speeches given by members of the family were therefore customarily leaden, delivered without tone or expression and couched in soporific officialese. This was, and quite rightly, another case of the official stuffiness to which Philip took exception, but his style – friendly, often light-hearted and with shafts of elegant wit or bursts of schoolboy humour – brought a new era to royal communications. This acted as a welcome counterweight to press reports of his irritated outbursts. His swearing was probably not as bad as that of King George V (few people's was!), but it was much more widely reported.

Many of the addresses he gave were in aid of organizations of which he was titular head, and here too there was to be no question that he would not be fully engaged. As he had told the NPFA when they asked him to take the presidency: 'I want to assure you that I have no intention of being a sitting tenant in this post.' How true that proved. For the NPFA, he proceeded to spend a period of time working in their London headquarters. Though he promised to be an active president of numerous organizations, he nevertheless did not want to be a permanent one. His notion was that after too many years at the helm staleness would set in. He would give whatever he had to offer for a few years and then make way for someone else. One example was the Maritime Trust, of which he was a founder member and served from 1967 to 1970. He was passionate about this field of endeavour (the organization rescues derelict ships and restores them), but three years was enough.

RIGHT: The Queen consort of Spain, Victoria Eugenie of Battenberg, left, together with the Countess and Count of Barcelona, are seen leaving Claridges Hotel for the wedding dance.

In November 1948 the couple's first child, Prince Charles, was born. He was delivered at Buckingham Palace while his father played squash with Michael Parker, Philip and Elizabeth's equerry. This was simply Philip's way of dealing with tension, and it was commonly felt back then that husbands would just be in the way at a birth.

By that time Philip had been in service overseas for a year. Having passed his staff college course, he had gone back to sea for the first time in five years. He was posted to the Mediterranean Fleet, which was based in Malta. Lord Mountbatten was already there as commander of a cruiser squadron. It seems difficult to believe that in those days the Navy was big enough to be able to afford to base an entire fleet in the peaceful Mediterranean. Philip was to serve as 1st Lieutenant aboard HMS *Chequers*.

It was a wonderful posting, and it would be a blessed interlude for the young officer and his wife, with whom he was able to spend a surprising amount of time. Elizabeth was busy not only with public duties but with Prince Charles. Yet she felt strongly that she wanted to share in his career insofar as her unique circumstances would allow. Her father agreed that she should be with her husband, but it was believed that the climate would not be suitable for their infant son, and Charles was therefore left with his grandparents. In 1950, Elizabeth had to return home to give birth to their daughter Anne. Philip went back for the child's christening. He took with him – in a kind and much-appreciated gesture – his locally recruited steward Vincent to attend the ceremony. The Maltese were charmed – and so were the wives of his colleagues in the Navy, for pieces of the christening cake were sent out for the families of the officers, petty officers and ratings messes.

Though he could not live in complete normality, Philip would have loved the escape his duties gave him from tiresome Palace routine. He was now in the company of like-minded men, doing a job he loved, and living in one of the most pleasant settings that the British Empire could provide. After years amid the drabness of post-war Britain, this sun-kissed Mediterranean island must have seemed like the Garden of Eden. He was stimulated by the challenges of his job, which, at a time that was largely uneventful, involved either training exercises or flag-showing visits. He also found a suitable outlet for energy by taking up polo.

Philip needed to take an exam to achieve promotion. These had not, as we have seen, been any obstacle to him in the past. He worked with his usual zeal and he did characteristically well – except in the subjects of ASDIC (anti-submarine sonar) and torpedo. He was failed. When Philip got wind that the Commander-in-Chief had considered overruling this decision because of who he was, he was livid. Since childhood he had been self-contained to a fault. It was an article of faith with him that he could succeed on his own merits in any competition he entered, and that he could earn his way without needing to call upon his position. Though naturally the fact that he had failed an exam he had expected to pass was irritating, it did not annoy him half as much as the notion that rules would be bent in his favour. He would quit the Navy, he said, if anyone tampered with his result. They didn't, he re-sat, and passed on the second attempt.

The year after arriving in Malta, he therefore achieved the ambition of all young naval officers and was given his own ship. Promoted Lieutenant Commander, he took over the frigate HMS *Magpie*. The ship made a number of courtesy visits, sometimes with the Princess on board, and this languid progress round the Mediterranean earned *Magpie* the nickname 'Edinburgh's private yacht'. The captain remained as generally, if not always universally, popular with ratings as he had been during the war. He was, in fact, a commander in the tradition of Hornblower – square-jawed, decisive, firm but kindly, taking no nonsense and punishing where necessary, yet displaying a noisy sense of humour and an ability to bring out the best in his men. His crew either loved or hated him, as would be the case among all those with whom he lived or worked, though his nickname among them – 'Dukey' – suggests a certain affection.

TOP RIGHT: The many wedding gifts given to Princess Elizabeth after her marriage to Philip, on display at St James's Palace, 1947.

BOTTOM RIGHT: A model of the royal state coach from M. Jean de Blieux of Paris, and a bride doll from F. F. Gardel among the many wedding gifts given to Princess Elizabeth after her marriage to Philip, on display at St James Palace, 1947.

As competitive as he had been on the playing fields of Cheam or Gordonstoun, he entered all inter-ship or inter-flotilla competitions with enthusiasm and drove his crew to win. *Magpie* duly became cock of the fleet and able to hoist the trophy – a wooden cockerel. Morale aboard was excellent, and the knowledge that the captain was married to the heir to the throne will have added to the sense of swagger among her crew.

Life ashore was equally rewarding. Princess Elizabeth joined him for months on end, though she often had to return home to deputize for her father, who was experiencing a worrying degree of ill health. Nevertheless, the couple stayed in the official residence of the Mountbattens in Malta, which the Admiral had vacated for them. The Princess, who after all was not abroad but in territory ruled by her father, was able to drive herself around, visit local shops with a minimum of fuss, and attend polo matches or cinemas (where she and Philip sat in the back row). She had never experienced such informality, and she was to treasure the memory, as was he.

A normal naval career would have involved more of what they had found, and so much enjoyed, in Malta – exotic postings, different commands, varied experience and scattered friendships – but Philip knew perfectly well that he could not hope for normality. His work kept being interrupted. In the autumn of 1951, he had to travel home with his wife. In the years after the war, the King had wanted to go to each dominion as a means of thanking his subjects for their support. South Africa had been visited, and now it was Canada's turn.

The trip was planned, but when the time came his health was simply not up to it. His daughter and her husband would go in his place. There was not time to make a lengthy voyage and, at Philip's suggestion, they flew the Atlantic instead, becoming the first Royals to do so (it was while visiting the cockpit during this innovatory journey that he conceived the desire to learn to fly himself). As they would do for many later official visits, they studied maps and textbooks, and were briefed by experts, to learn in advance as much as they could about the country. They were also to make a southward swing to Washington to see President Truman. This was their first official visit to a foreign head of state, and the avuncular President was an easy man to impress. Like his countrymen he was charmed by Elizabeth's youth and beauty and by Philip's manliness and sense of humour. He would not be the last to take this view. On the couple's return, King George was sufficiently pleased with their efforts to make them both Privy Councillors.

He also gave them a further task. They were to undertake another, and longer, overseas tour, this time travelling across Africa, sailing to Ceylon (now Sri Lanka) and then continuing to Australia and New Zealand. Once again this was a visit that the King and Queen should have made, but King George's health rendered it too much of a risk. Philip had to take indefinite leave from the Navy to meet such a level of commitment. Though there would be pleasure in seeing once again some old haunts (his wartime service had taken him to both Ceylon and Australia), a crowded official visit may have seemed poor compensation for the curtailment of the most enjoyable spell of naval duty he had known.

What followed is well known. A few days into the journey, while he and Elizabeth stayed with their entourage on a Kenyan game reserve, the King died in his sleep at Sandringham. As of the night of 5 February 1952, Princess Elizabeth was Queen. Tidings of her father's death reached her somewhat erratically. The Palace could not contact her, and the news was first picked up on the radio by one of the journalists who was accompanying the party, and was at a hotel some distance away. From him it went to Martin Charteris, the Princess's private secretary, and thence to Michael Parker. Parker made the announcement to Philip, who told his wife and then took her for a walk in the nearby gardens to share a few moments of privacy. Parker, an old naval colleague of Philip, knew how profoundly this would affect his friend's

RIGHT: Princess Elizabeth and Philip hold their first child Prince Charles, aged six months.

LEFT: The King and Queen
with Princess Margaret
at London Airport to
say goodbye to Princess
Elizabeth and Philip as they
leave for their Australia
tour. This is one of the last
photographs ever taken of
the King.

future. He later remarked that: 'I never felt so sorry for anyone in my life. He looked as if you'd dropped half the world on him.'

And it was not, of course, only Philip who knew how completely different everything would now be. For the new Queen it must have been like hearing that the world had ended. It is difficult for those of us outside the family to appreciate the tragedy of this event. Not only would there have been the loss to cope with of a parent whom the Princess had adored and idolized, and the sense of guilt – not uncommon among sons and daughters – at not having been there when it happened. There was also the stark knowledge that her own private life was over. From the moment she received the news, she was head of state and her time was no longer her own. She must abandon at once not only the journey that she was so much enjoying and the visits to other countries that she had been about to see for the first time, but the whole concept of further years as a naval wife.

Philip would have understood all this. He would have seen his career in the Service evaporate in the space of those few minutes. How fortunate for him, and for the monarchy, that he was both strong and devoid of introspection. He would have absorbed the situation and at once set about the practicalities of getting his wife home and helping her prepare for what was to come – the grief, the funeral, the sudden wealth of new tasks, even the immediate move from their newly refurbished home at Clarence House.

Elizabeth shared his sense of practicality. There was nothing to be gained by simply worrying. While her father had burst into tears at the thought of taking over the throne – and he was by no means the first monarch in history to do that – Elizabeth was quietly firm. She settled at once the question of what name she would use ('My own, of course – what else?'), and showed regret not for her own anguish but for those others whose arrangements had been thrown into confusion by the sudden change of plan.

She would for several years – since the King's first serious illness – have been mentally preparing herself for such an eventuality. Travelling with her in the luggage was a Royal Standard, as well as a letter to both Houses of Parliament and black mourning clothes, precisely in case these should be needed. The latter were routinely packed (but had already been shipped ahead and could not be retrieved), the two former were brought along because of the King's state of health, as they had been on the trip to Canada. She was to say that she was fortunate in that, while her mother and sister (who had been at Sandringham when the King passed away) had nothing but grieving to fill their time, she had the distraction of learning her new role.

On that February morning, Philip's status changed forever. Previously he had been the head of the family even though his wife had outranked him. Now he would take up the familiar role in which the public would become accustomed to seeing him, walking a few paces behind her; standing in the background, hands behind his back, as she declared a building open or presented a trophy; smiling at the humour in a speech she delivered; accompanying, and making conversation with, the wives of a thousand presidents or mayors or generals or company directors while the Queen walked ahead with their husbands.

He fitted into this secondary role with apparent effortlessness and with overwhelming success. A man of self-evidently wide interests and considerable abilities, accustomed to dominating the environments in which he found himself, he quickly learned to fade into the background when in public with his wife. Yet he was always ready to help along a stalled conversation, to enliven with some jocular remark a formal, momentary silence. To spot in a crowd some person, or something, to which the Queen's attention could be drawn to create interest or humour. He was good at all this from the beginning.

RIGHT: Princess Elizabeth, with Philip, takes the salute as 1,200 members of the Boys Brigade Council march past at Balmoral Castle.

CHAPTER SIX

A ROYAL CONSORT

PREVIOUS SPREAD: The Duke of Edinburgh holds the Queen's hand after she delivers the speech at the State Opening of Parliament in the House of Lords in London.

TOP: Philip at the Coronation at Westminster Abbey.

BOTTOM: Queen Elizabeth II, wearing the Imperial State Crown, and Philip, in the uniform of Admiral of the Fleet, wave from the balcony to the crowds around the gates of Buckingham Palace after the Coronation.

The Queen was to give him as much leeway as the circumstances of their unusual life permitted. He was allowed to run the family, as he had before her accession, making the important decisions about their children's education, while she ruled the country.

The couple moved from their home at Clarence House. They did this with extreme reluctance, because their first home had been specially renovated for them and, though it is a huge building, it seemed positively cosy compared to the Palace. They also took up residence at Windsor Castle where Philip, not one to be awed by history, occupied the study used by Edward VII. He was eminently at home in this place, among the trophies of a thousand years of the Royal Family. When asked if he found such a setting strange or overwhelming, he answered laconically that his mother had been born there. He was to make his presence felt in the Castle, too. He redesigned the unattractive garden on which the family's windows look out, creating with the help of an artist a more sympathetic layout. Perhaps more significantly, it was at his suggestion that some state dinners were moved from Buckingham Palace to Windsor. These have proved a magnificent experience for those who attend them. The visitors are transferred from cars to carriages for the journey up the Long Walk – the lengthy straight road that leads through Windsor Great Park. They travel with outriders, grooms and a cavalry escort. Entering the Castle quadrangle, they find a detachment of the Foot Guards drawn up awaiting inspection. Later, they attend the banquet itself in St George's Hall, at a table so long that they can scarcely see the farther end of it. It is surely the most splendid setting on earth in which to eat, an experience that money cannot buy. Philip's sense of occasion has been responsible for creating something truly magical.

He was a member of the Coronation Commission – the body that planned, over long months and in consultation with the many organizations involved – the ceremony at which his wife would be crowned. He attended the Abbey in the cocked hat and blue-and-gold uniform of an Admiral of the Fleet and was the first of her noblemen to swear allegiance to her once the unwieldy St Edward's Crown had been set on her head. With her accession, her husband had gone in a matter of a few short months from the rank of Commander – equivalent to a Lieutenant Colonel in the Army – to that of Admiral of the Fleet. He had vaulted over men with lengthier service and greater experience to reach the top of the ladder of promotion. Yet because he had not earned this status it will have been a source of frustration rather than pride. He had simultaneously become a Field Marshal and a Marshal of the Royal Air Force. All he could do was to wear the uniforms and do his best to live up to such positions.

Despite all his reading about Prince Albert, Philip had no real pattern to follow with regard to his role. He was to quip that, 'Constitutionally I don't exist,' and this was true. He was obliged to find a function that would keep him occupied and show the public he was earning the money they paid him through the Civil List. He had already begun accumulating a collection of trusteeships, presidencies, patronages and honorary positions, both military and civilian, and these swelled into a flood now his wife had become Queen. Though he would accept invitations to speak or to visit, he did not accept every post that he was invited to fill. He considered carefully what he might be able to contribute to the various organizations. Once in office, he was quite capable of sending letters of enquiry, or even tetchy notes, requesting explanations, clarifications, amplification of minor points – a host of things that showed he had read the small print of annual reports or secretaries' letters. His visits, to offices or events, were like military inspections (perhaps not surprising, in view of his background), in which he would stalk around asking penetrating questions and catching out those who were not prepared. He had seemingly limitless energy and curiosity.

Though he did many things well, he was not universally popular. He was seen as a thorn in the side by courtiers, for he had a certain

RIGHT: Princess Elizabeth and Philip (background) leaving the 'Duke of Edinburgh' hotel at Victoria during a visit to Gozo.

TOP: Princess Elizabeth
and Philip watch
stonemasons cutting huge
blocks of stone at a quarry
on the island of Gozo.

BOTTOM: Princess
Elizabeth arrives in
Malta for a visit. There,
with Philip to greet the
Princess, was the Governor
Sir Gerald Creasy and his
wife.

impatience with what he was memorably to christen 'fundungus' —
accumulated custom that carried on simply because it always had and
regardless of whether it was of any visible benefit to anyone. He was
keen to modernize the institution and he was a man of strong mind and
strong character, but he was often up against formidable opposition.

He was perceived to have great influence over the Queen and in
some respects he undoubtedly did, but in matters of kingship and
tradition she took her cue not from her husband but from her parents.
She did not want to do things differently to the way her father had
done them. She wanted to ensure as much continuity as possible
between his reign and hers. The senior Queen Elizabeth, who was an
even more jealous guardian of King George's legacy, was a very strong
character indeed, and could effectively obstruct changes of which she
did not approve. 'What will Mummy say?' was a catchphrase of the
Queen's throughout her mother's life, and the notion of her displeasure
was more than once to frustrate Philip's designs. This extended even to
improvements on royal estates. He wanted to reorganize the domestic
landscape — lawns and shrubs — that surrounded Sandringham, yet he
gave up the notion because the Queen Mother let it be known that she
was happy with the existing vista.

His behaviour also caused some disquiet outside the family. He
had always been accustomed to relaxing with the same enthusiasm
he devoted to work, and like many young husbands he had a number
of friends from his bachelor days who did not fit comfortably into
his new life. He continued to see them, however, particularly in the
setting of the Thursday Club — a loose gathering of men from media,
military and cultural circles, whose boisterous and often puerile
humour found an outlet in regular lunches. The members included the
actor James Robertson Justice and Baron, the society photographer.
Their gatherings could be riotous and Philip was sometimes seen in
the company of members — and of women — at London nightclubs.
Rumours of flirtation would surface periodically in the press, fuelling
a perception of him as somewhat raffish. While Elizabeth's behaviour,

both as Princess and as Queen, had never given reporters anything to seize upon, Philip caused some offence among his wife's more moralistic subjects by going 'out on the town' without her. He also brought opprobrium on himself, in the eyes of the Lord's Day Observance Society, by playing polo on Sundays.

The Queen has never told him what he may or may not do, and has tried to compensate him for his loss of independence. She created him a Prince of the United Kingdom – thus finalizing his title as Prince Philip, Duke of Edinburgh, and agreed that the surname adopted by non-inheriting members of her family should be Mountbatten-Windsor. She was aware that he found frustrating the restricted life they led. He was energetic, intelligent and restless. All the skills that he had learned in the Navy – in organizing and running the small community of a ship – were rusting away through disuse, and it is perhaps understandable that he sought to exercise them on the Royal Household. Because he had no role, the press gave the impression that he was wandering about the Palace all day looking for ways to overhaul the doubtless archaic and protocol-bound ways in which the household was run. It was reported that he had descended on the kitchens and made a time-and-motion study of the work done there. It was further rumoured that this would lead to the sacking of members of staff. In the event, he was to state that several more staff had been taken on as a result of his findings.

Philip had become a kind of schoolboy's hero, a gentleman-amateur sportsman and explorer. He had taken up flying despite concern on the part of Whitehall, and he pursued this hobby with the same zeal he had devoted to polo or to pulling whalers in naval races. He crammed in hours of flight training whenever his schedule would allow. Often snatching a single spare hour out of an already hectic day, he progressed steadily from training aircraft to a range of large planes. And when he had got the hang of fixed-wing flying, he started again on helicopters, having had to persuade the Prime Minister, Winston Churchill, to let

TOP RIGHT: Prince Philip walks out on to the pitch at Dean Park, Bournemouth, for the match between the Duke's County Players Team and Hampshire in aid of the National Playing Fields Association.

BOTTOM RIGHT: Prince Philip taking part in a polo match at the Nyeri Polo Club, Kenya, whilst accompanying Princess Elizabeth on a Royal Tour of the Commonwealth.

TOP LEFT: Princess
Elizabeth enjoys a stroll
with her husband. This
was their first public
appearance since their
wedding.

BOTTOM LEFT: Princess
Elizabeth and Philip go
by carriage to Waterloo
Station for their train to
Winchester for the start of
their honeymoon.

him pursue such a potentially risky hobby. He had of course wanted to join the RAF before he settled on the Navy. And in the field of flying he was able to do what he had always sought to do – to compete on equal terms and win his successes through skill and practice. Between December 1952 and the spring of 1955 he went from initial flying of a Chipmunk training aircraft to the more complex Harvard, and then graduated to the Oxford, and ultimately to the Provost. After moving on to flying helicopters came the wings of the Royal Navy, after which he earned the equivalent status with the Army Air Corps. Then he learned to handle jet aircraft – the Vampire and the Meteor.

This was serious flying. He had moved a long way from a mere hobby – but then he was fortunate in that most weekend pilots do not happen to hold the highest ranks in the Services or have access, whenever they wish it, to the resources of a military airbase. Even among the civilian pilots aboard commercial airliners his name, of course, worked magic. Should he be flying as passenger in a Trident or a Boeing he would naturally have been accorded the courtesy of an invitation to visit the cockpit. Once there it was but a short step to having a go at the controls. He clearly knew what he was doing, and equally he enjoyed the shop-talk and professional banter of the crew. He was able to make a pleasure out of what otherwise have been very dreary hours of travel. Altogether he was to pile up more than 6,000 hours of flying time. In an aerial age few things could more effectively have cemented Prince Philip's reputation as a modern, technocratic royal than this love of flying.

An escape from many of the things that bedevilled him – the disapproval of older Palace officials, the fact of being stuck ashore when he longed to be at sea, even the vagaries of the English climate – was offered him in 1956. This was more or less at the time that the 'seven year itch' is common among husbands. He was to open the Olympic Games that year in Melbourne, Australia, and he would go there, with his old friend and now private secretary Michael Parker, on HMY *Britannia*, which was a new vessel at that time. The 35,000-mile journey could be seen as a sort of proving voyage, testing not the ship's engines but its role as a floating palace. As plans advanced for the trip, Philip conceived the idea of adding stops in other territories that, because of their small size or remoteness, had never had such a visit. The map of the Southern Hemisphere is dotted with British dependencies: British Antarctic Territory, the Falkland Islands, Tristan da Cunha, St Helena. Philip believed it was important to show an interest in these far-flung peoples and places.

The royal yacht was a splendid example of modern technology – a wonder of the age (Philip has compared it with the cathedrals of old as a symbol of the times in which it was built) – and Philip had, at the suggestion of King George, been involved in its design. The people of the Southern Hemisphere could not easily travel to London and therefore royalty – and one of its palaces – would come to them. Could he have carried out such visits by some quicker means of transport, such as by plane? No. More than sixty years later, St Helena and Tristan da Cunha still have no airports.

With and without the Queen, Philip has travelled more miles than any member of the family. He has used all manner of transport and been photographed in an immense variety of strange garb, receiving honorary membership of communities that have ranged from universities and city livery companies to the native tribes of Fiji and New Zealand and Africa. In pidgin English he has a title: 'Number One Fallah Belong Missis Queen' and, bizarrely, he is worshipped as a god by one remote tribe, which celebrates his birthday every year.

His tour was a great success for the inhabitants of the territories he visited. They not only saw the Queen's husband – often resplendent in naval uniform – but also something of the trappings that went with royalty. A Royal Marine band was aboard, and their beating retreat was – as it always is – a splendid and moving spectacle. The yacht's crew played football against the Tristan islanders (the result was a 2–2 draw). The Duke heard umpteen renditions of the national anthem

TOP RIGHT: Philip is seen trying the passenger's seat of the new 3.5-litre Jaguar XKSS sports car during his visit to the Motor Industry Research Association's headquarters near Nuneaton, Warwickshire.

BOTTOM RIGHT: The Queen and her husband, Prince Philip, on the foredeck of the SS *Gothic* just off the coast of Tonga.

and received hosts of Loyal Addresses, inspected scouts and brownies, visited schools and hospitals, and read the lessons in church services. In between landfalls there were long days of deck-hockey, birdwatching and painting. Like some eighteenth-century nobleman on the Grand Tour, Philip had taken with him on his odyssey an artist, Edward Seago, whose record of the voyage inspired Philip's own work in oils. Both came back after four months with impressively full portfolios.

Philip was deeply irritated, however, to return and find two things. One was that the press had decided to portray his travels as a sort of schoolboy outing – a 'jolly' – that had been largely devoted to sightseeing and shipboard games. His absence had been so long that one newspaper headline read, sarcastically: 'Prince Philip visits Britain.' The other issue was that his long absence had brought a rash of rumours that his marriage was in trouble. He stated, with a hint of resentment, that, 'I believe there are some things for which it is worth making some personal sacrifice, and I believe that the British Commonwealth is one of those things.'

While the public was accustomed to his interest in the air, and in sea-travel aboard an ultra-modern yacht, at home he was also seen as modern. He disliked, for instance, the practice of Palace footmen wearing powdered hair and had it discontinued. This was the era of presentations at Court – the formal introduction of upper-class young women into society by having them briefly introduced to the Queen. However much the mothers of the girls may have enjoyed these occasions, for some participants they must have been an ordeal, and the widely believed rumour that Philip only smiled at the ugly ones cannot have done much to calm their nerves. Whatever he really thought of them – and they are likely to have offended his sense of practical modernity – he was certainly influential in having these annual occasions replaced. Instead, an additional garden party and informal lunches were created, to which not young ladies but a cross section of those who contributed to the life of the nation was invited. This change had less to do with a sense of modernity than with his own impatience. Prince Philip preferred meeting interesting people with whom he could engage in serious talk over the lunch table. He also enjoyed the notion of putting together a random collection of successful men and women and seeing how they related to each other.

He could not have shaken off, even if he had wanted to, the image of a glorified scoutmaster – especially when he was always issuing 'challenges' to the young and vigorous. In one of many instances, he urged students to have a go at working their way round the world for £5. This outlook made him an ideal figure to act as the public face of a new venture that was begun on the suggestion of his old headmaster Dr Hahn. Philip was much involved with setting up the scheme that became The Duke of Edinburgh's Award. When launched in 1956, it was only for boys, and resembled the activities that had filled the spare time of Gordonstoun pupils for years. Within two years it had been opened to girls and its scope had widened beyond camping weekends or the conquering of mountain peaks to include such indoor activities as mastering a foreign language or learning to throw pots.

The scheme quickly spread abroad. Given not only its universal, non-political nature but Philip's position in the Commonwealth, it was inevitable that this would happen. In the UK he was a regular visitor to camps and other activities – questioning, encouraging and joking with those who took part. They achieved bronze, silver and gold awards, and a surprising number of them became addicted to achievement throughout their lives. For those who reached the highest stage, they were invited to the Palace (Holyrood for the Scots and Buckingham for everyone else) to receive it, and there would be the familiar hallmarks of a meeting with him: the piercing look, the avuncular handshake, the blunt questioning, the gruff laughter as they told of some misadventure.

While the scheme was a useful enough idea to have succeeded without his patronage, he added immensely to its appeal. His philosophy, whether with reference to his own children or others, has

RIGHT: The Queen, the Duke of Edinburgh, Queen Elizabeth the Queen Mother, and Princess Margaret.

been the same. He believes that success is infectious. Win in one field and it gives you a habit of winning – an expectation of reaching your objective – that will spill over into other areas of your life. The Award will also have taught valuable lessons about organizing your efforts and about developing stamina and persistence. Learn to cook, in other words, and it will help you learn to sky-dive, paint in oils or do the tango.

Another aspect that has been important to Philip since the Queen succeeded has been the farming of the royal estates. At the beginning of her reign this was something just waiting for his energy and reforming zeal. For a sailor, he took very readily to life on the land, but then his gift was for organizing, rationalizing, brainstorming and coming up with better and more efficient ways of doing things. He developed the dairy herd at Windsor, began the growing of Christmas trees there as a commercial crop, and took up chicken farming in earnest – though by battery methods which would later become unpopular. At Sandringham, where the estate contains considerable amounts of agricultural land, he decided to go in for serious commercial farming in a place where the family had previously thought only in terms of leisure, and had done little more than shoot birds. The produce of these lands was, first and foremost, intended to feed the Royals and their household. This helped to keep down the cost of the monarchy to taxpayers and a surplus was soon built up which could be sold to the public or to the food industry. He converted disused buildings into a giant piggery that went on to produce bacon on what was almost a minor industrial scale, and oversaw the farming, of among other things, lavender, as well as blackcurrants which, he tells visitors, are bought by Ribena.

Reaching middle age, he remained as attached as ever to the outdoors, and had become notably interested in birds. He was asked to serve as President of the World Wildlife Fund, despite objections in some quarters that he enjoyed shooting pheasant and stalking stags.

His attitude to game has always been the pragmatic approach of a countryman – that animal populations need to be kept down and that some creatures cause so much damage that they need to be controlled. Interestingly, he never took to foxhunting, that most English of blood sports, though this was clearly not on any moral grounds. The WWF wanted him because he was enthusiastic about its aims, because his international profile would raise awareness of the organization, and because he was known to take an active rather than a passive interest in the causes with which he became involved. He was also a very articulate and persuasive speaker whose words would influence. He proved as tireless a champion as had been hoped, attending conferences, giving addresses, visiting countries and talking to governments.

A further strand of his life involved an activity of which the public knew next to nothing. In the 1970s he was a member of a committee that oversaw the standardizing of rules for a number of sports. During one meeting, a man mused aloud, 'I suppose we ought to have rules for carriage driving.' 'I've never heard of it,' said Philip, who then became interested enough to learn more about it. Having given up first cricket and then polo as a result of advancing years, he was looking for something else, and this was a skilled activity that would require a steady hand and tight control over not one horse but a team. Carriage driving is not a race. The object is – as in showjumping – to tackle a series of obstacles, such as steep banks and streams, with precision, winning points for precise cornering or steady speed and losing them for straying off the route or scraping against the barriers. One or more passengers are carried and the distribution of their weight is crucial to the stability of the light vehicle as it swerves and pitches in the uneven terrain. Philip found immense satisfaction in this. He was able to keep in training at both Windsor and Sandringham and to compete in contests throughout the country.

His public manner remained relaxed, but with increasing age his reputation changed from that of wit to curmudgeon. While earlier in the reign his comments, quips and the asides in his innumerable

RIGHT: Philip (left) takes part in the Pony-Four-in-Hand.

LEFT: The Queen and
Prince Philip in the gold
State Coach, which was
built in 1728. On the way
to the Queen's Coronation
almost 200 years later, they
listened to the coverage
of the event on a radio
concealed inside.

speeches were seen as amusing, his humour is now often considered
crass. When Prince Philip is mentioned, the word 'gaffe' is seldom far
from people's minds. The perception is widespread that he is incapable
of restraining a sharp, often insensitive and hurtful sense of humour.
He is thought to say things that are damaging to the Royal Family and
even to the country.

Sometimes, admittedly, his comments do come within this
category. His most notoriously frank comment was one which he made
in an interview for American television in 1969, when he stated, with
regard to royal finances and the Civil List allowances on which he and
other members of the family lived: 'We go into the red next year. I shall
probably have to give up polo.' This remark caused outrage at home. It
is a rule for politicians – and anyone else officially representing Britain
– never to criticize the country while they are outside it. To make a
statement about the funds on which he lived – sums that sound more
than generous to those on lower incomes – was seen as insensitive. To
suggest that a need to economize might cause him to give up a very
expensive and socially exclusive sport might well have added insult to
injury. Though he was the one Royal who has genuine experience of
working in a profession and moving among all sorts and conditions of
men, his utterances were something of a propaganda coup for socialists
and anti-monarchists.

Another instance was during a state visit to India, in which he and
the Queen were at Amritsar. This town was the scene of a notorious
incident in April 1919. A peaceful protest by locals against British
rule in the subcontinent was seen by the local commander, Brigadier
Reginald Dyer, as a riot. Troops were ordered to open fire and, as
the crowd tried to flee, between 400 and 500 people were killed
(estimates vary). Though Dyer was found guilty by court martial and
forced to retire (in other words, even the British authorities agreed
that he had overreacted), Indian nationalists kept a sense of angry
grievance at fever pitch. The incident still arouses strong feeling in the
country, and it was speculated that the Queen would formally offer

an apology for it on her visit. She didn't, though she spoke of it with regret. The Duke, seeing an inscription that gave the number of dead, said loudly enough to be overheard: 'That's wrong. I was in the Navy with Dyer's son.' His hosts, under such circumstances, would not have said anything, but the accompanying press trumpeted the story and the usual reactions, from head shaking to outrage, were the result.

In this case he of course would have meant no calculated insult – he has throughout his whole adult life been involved with international diplomacy, and knows its rules. His remark will have been spontaneous, and he was merely questioning the accuracy of a statement that, displayed in public in a highly emotional setting, he considered to be exaggerated for political purposes.

In less serious circumstances, where the potential for damage is less, he will often be motivated by a sense of mischief. Not everything he says is a thoughtless, let-slip comment; rather, it is evidence of a wicked sense of fun. He likes to provoke. 'Who are you?' he might brusquely demand of a self-important junior minister. The trouble starts when he is overheard by people who themselves have no sense of humour. The Queen herself undoubtedly possesses a similarly irreverent view of some of the people and places she encounters. In private she is known to have a sharp sense of humour and a gift for mimicry, and is rumoured to be able to 'take off' with surprising accuracy some of the public figures she has met.

Sometimes public reaction to his 'gaffes' is unexpected. It is refreshing when, instead of the usual grumbling, the public sides with him. His notorious comments in America about having to give up polo actually caused a number of dockers in a Bermondsey pub to open a fund to buy him a new pony. His reaction was typical, what one would expect of a National Playing Fields Association president – he thanked them for the gesture but suggested they devote the money to doing something for the young, rather than the middle-aged.

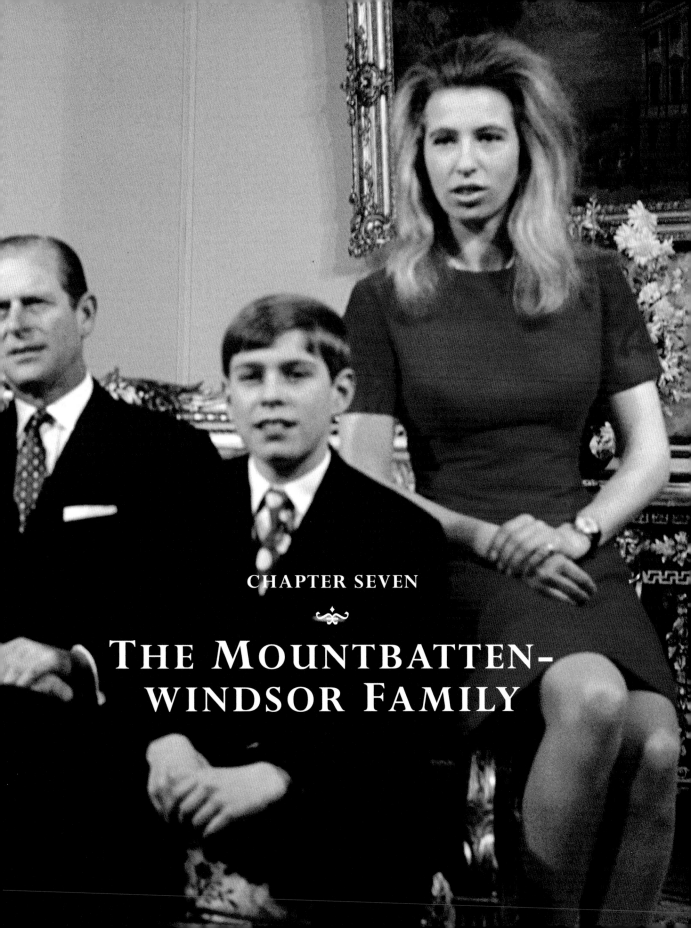

CHAPTER SEVEN

THE MOUNTBATTEN-WINDSOR FAMILY

As a parent, Philip is believed to have been strict. It is public perception that he loomed over the upbringing of his four children (Charles 1948, Anne 1950, Andrew 1960, Edward 1964): forceful, exacting, disappointed with the slightest failing, leaving them with a permanent sense of inadequacy. Is this true?

Only in part. Yes, he was an ambitious parent, but it can be argued that any good parent is. He wanted them to do well, to build and maintain confidence. He was well aware that they would be scrutinized throughout their lives and that they would suffer greater humiliations than others if they failed. He therefore set high standards. These included, incidentally, making them apologize to Palace staff if they had spoken rudely to them or put them to unnecessary trouble. Many references, however, exist to his gentleness and consideration in encouraging his children, and to his showing understanding in adverse moments. His was, of course, a difficult legacy to live up to. His sons would not grow up to be so tall, or so handsome. Neither Charles nor Andrew, who were cadets at Dartmouth, won the King's Dirk. The fact that, in terms of leisure pursuits, father and son liked to do similar things did not help, for wherever Charles went his father seemed already to have been there, setting the bar dispiritingly high.

When Prince Edward, the youngest and shyest of the sons, took what seemed an uncharacteristic step and joined the Royal Marines after graduating from Cambridge, his father (who was and is the Captain General of the Corps) must have been very proud. When Edward chose to leave without completing the training programme because he found that his heart was not in it, there will undoubtedly have been some disappointed anger on Philip's part. He is not someone who would allow himself to give up on a challenge, and he would have seen this as a failure by Edward to 'pull himself together'. What might be considered even worse was that the Prince sought a career on the fringes of show business, enlisting as a general factotum in Andrew Lloyd Webber's theatre company to learn the business from the ground up. However laudable this may have been, it is unlikely to have been the future that his father envisaged for him.

Edward is, however, his favourite among his children. It is Edward who has taken over the running of the Duke of Edinburgh's Award, and Edward who, after Philip's death, will be created the next Duke of Edinburgh. The two are visibly fond of each other. Anyone who expected Philip never to speak to his son again when he left the Marines had misunderstood, for Philip admires people who plough their own furrow. Such is his reputation for explosive disapproval that the whole nation had seemed to be vicariously bracing itself for his outburst of indignation, and yet none came. He is actually much more sensitive than people expect.

In fact, Prince Philip is thoroughly fed up with the references – which still appear – to his demanding nature as a father. Though he certainly pushed his children to achieve as much as they could, he was deeply caring. When they were infants he was punctilious in devoting time to bathing and reading to them.

His daughter displays a nature that can be as brusque and barking as his own, and his three sons have – consciously or otherwise – modelled their public manner on his. Their way of walking with hands behind backs, the tone of voice in which they ask questions, their witticisms and exclamations of surprise owe much to him and were likely absorbed by osmosis rather than studied. Charles is most like him in this respect, though their natures are of course very dissimilar.

Philip planned his children's education. Because the Queen was responsible for ruling over the state, she wished Philip to have authority within the family. It was he who decided that the children would attend schools as he had, rather than have tuition at home from a governess, as had been the case with Elizabeth. He decided that Charles's education would copy his own – a spell at Cheam, and then Gordonstoun (which Andrew and Edward would also attend). It was not just that the latter school had given him a good grounding

RIGHT: Princess Elizabeth and Philip with their baby daughter, Princess Anne, after her christening at Buckingham Palace. The baby, given the names Anne Elizabeth Alice Louise, wore the royal robe of Honiton lace handed down from Queen Victoria's days.

in life (he was not as devoted an old boy as is sometimes suggested, though he has given money towards new buildings) but that he believed in Dr Hahn's vision. He considered Charles to be somewhat too sensitive, and sought to toughen him up. He wanted the heir to the throne to mix with a variety of pupils, to learn to endure cold and discomfort, to take as his leisure pursuits the same sailing and cricket and to gain the same satisfaction from manning a coastguard station.

The school was a mistake. Charles did achieve one or two points of similarity: he too became Guardian, and like Philip he appeared in a production of *Macbeth* – playing the king, rather than the more minor role of Donalbain. Otherwise their experiences were as widely different as their backgrounds. Charles did not have Philip's physical or mental toughness, his self-sufficiency or even his propensity for making noise. He was homesick and he was bullied, and when his time was up he escaped rather thankfully. Though he kept silent for many years about his experiences, his biographers – and notably Jonathan Dimbleby, to whom he talked with great frankness in the early 1990s – have been unanimous in conveying the impression that he was a sensitive soul cast into a lions' den.

Philip has been more wounded by these accusations than the public probably realize. He and the Queen strongly believe that they did their best for all their children and, like the parents of many who grow up and speak or write about their formative years, they do not recognize themselves in the stories they hear of aloofness, preoccupation and over-strictness. Philip has said in interview that, 'He's a romantic – and I am a pragmatist,' adding wearily, 'and because I don't see things as a romantic would, I'm unfeeling.'

There is no doubting the couple's fondness for their offspring. This was evident to anyone who saw the family together in the children's earlier years. Philip saw to it that they met interesting people, grew up without being spoiled (his presents to them at birthdays and Christmas were useful and modest) and learned consideration for the staff who looked after them. He wanted them to go away to school in order to learn the independence that this step usually teaches, and to accustom them to living somewhere other than in palaces. Gordonstoun had the advantage that he already knew the place and – this was important – that it was hundreds of miles from Fleet Street. This choice of school did not fit Charles's artistic personality, but both Andrew and Edward were happy enough there, and Anne was similarly content to go to Benenden. His plans worked out, in other words, in three instances out of four. It has in any case been suggested that Charles, mellowed by age and by his subsequent marriage to the woman he had loved all along, is today less critical of his father than was the case almost two decades ago.

Naturally, the passage of years brought family losses. In 1969 his mother, Princess Andrew of Greece, died at Buckingham Palace. She had been living there, as guest of her daughter-in-law and son, for several years. She was eighty-four. She had been an absolutely remarkable woman, chiefly notable for having founded her own order of Orthodox nuns, whose dove-grey habit she had designed herself and which she had worn to the Coronation. Deaf for decades, she had been expert in lip-reading and, in the days of silent films, had been able to entertain her family on visits to the cinema by telling them what the actors on screen were really saying during their dialogues (one man, in the midst of a love scene, was telling the woman that he was about to be evicted for not paying his rent). It was from his mother that Philip inherited much of his strong determination, while his father had given him his physical stature, his sense of humour and a good deal of his gruffness.

A further, and equally painful, loss came exactly a decade later when his Uncle Dickie was murdered by the IRA. Mountbatten had remained for the whole of his life a father-figure to Philip. He had not been close to George VI or to Queen Elizabeth (and this was in part because he had been an intimate of Edward VIII, George's banished

TOP: Making a happy group on the lawns at Balmoral are the Queen, Prince Philip, and their three children Princess Anne, Prince Charles and baby Prince Andrew, on his father's knee.

BOTTOM: The Prince of Wales, with his father (left) and Captain Iain Tennant, Chairman of the Gordonstoun Board of Governors, arriving at Gordonstoun for the Prince's first day at Public School.

brother) but he later became a valued friend to the Royal Family, particularly after the death of his wife Edwina in 1960. He was often photographed in their company, at polo matches, aboard HMY *Britannia* or at the Trooping the Colour (he was Colonel of the Life Guards, and therefore took part in this). He shared, of course, the enthusiasm for polo that was inherited by Philip and then by Charles. He filled much of the void in the family left by the premature death of King George. Having been an honorary father to Philip, he had become honorary grandfather to Philip's eldest son, and indeed was to be described in that precise term on the wreath that Charles would place on his coffin.

Born with the twentieth century, Mountbatten was very much an elder statesman by the late 1970s, not only within the British Royal Family but in the wider context of European royalty. He was a rare survivor of the pre-1914 age of kings – a world of courts and uniforms and endless relations – a symbol of vanished splendour. A nephew of Tsar Nicholas II, he had had a boyhood crush on the Grand Duchess Marie, one of the four beautiful daughters of the Tsar who had perished with the rest of that family at the hands of the Bolsheviks, and such a connection seemed almost unreal in a decade defined by punk rock and trade union militancy.

His association with historic grandeur had been further enhanced by the fact that he had been the last Viceroy of India, inhabiting a court of his own that was like something out of the Arabian Nights, and living in a palace that was the size of a railway terminus. He was more than simply a clotheshorse for uniforms, however, for he had had to make policy, and was responsible for decisions that affected many millions of people. He had been Supreme Allied Commander in South East Asia during the Second World War, and as such received the surrender of Japanese forces in Singapore. As Viceroy he had decided to bring forward the granting of independence to India, rushing through a highly complicated process that involved intricate negotiation. The resulting partition of the subcontinent brought a time of chaos and led to the dislocation of whole populations and the deaths of innumerable Muslims and Hindus. Opinion was divided as to whether Mountbatten had handled the issue well or badly. He himself had said that he would await the judgement of history. Although much opinion in the region itself was hostile to him, general feeling in Britain was that he had done the best in the circumstances, for the British had wanted a swift exit from their Empire anyway.

He was, in other words, the living history of a more spacious age, a status reflected in his elaborate uniforms and in the sizeable collection of orders and medals he had accumulated — he was so fond of these trappings that he took them with him on his travels in a specially designed case. He was still very active, and as he approached his eightieth birthday, press and publishers began to take stock of his life in print. He had long since planned his own funeral — a strange notion, but one in which royalty takes pleasure. 'I shall enjoy the fun of dying,' he said in a television interview.

He took his holidays in the Republic of Ireland, a neighbouring state that held a historic grudge against Britain because one of its four provinces — Ulster — remained by choice a part of the United Kingdom. Mountbatten's Irish home, Classiebawn Castle, was in the west of the country, a peaceful region far removed both geographically and spiritually from the troubled streets of Belfast. He had gone there every summer for many years with his children and grandchildren. The locals liked him, and no one expected harm to come to him. 'Who'd want to interfere with an old man on holiday,' he had said.

On 27 August 1979, the world found out. That morning, the small fishing boat in which he and his family were leaving the harbour was destroyed by an IRA bomb. He was killed, as were two of his relations and a local youth. It was an atrocity that shocked the world. He had the state funeral that he had so meticulously planned, but it was not the celebration he had envisaged. The nation had been expecting to lose him, but not so suddenly or so viciously.

TOP RIGHT: Prince William shows the Queen and Prince Philip the Sea King helicopter he flies during his training as a Search and Rescue pilot during a visit to RAF Valley in Anglesey.

BOTTOM RIGHT: Left to right: Prince Philip speaks to Prince William and Prince Harry at Royal Military Academy Sandhurst after The Sovereign's Parade that marked the completion of Prince Harry's Officer training.

For Philip, as for the rest of the family, this loss was devastating. Yet there was no public giving way to grieve. While the British press snarled insults at the IRA and at the Irish in general, the family behaved with a steely dignity. Prince Charles, summoned back to London by the event, deliberately drove himself in his open-top Aston Martin through the city, a conspicuous show of courage at a time when further terrorist assassinations could have been attempted at any time, and a gesture of which his great-uncle would surely have approved. Philip, reading the lesson in Westminster Abbey in a voice that did not even tremble, had now became the family's patriarch.

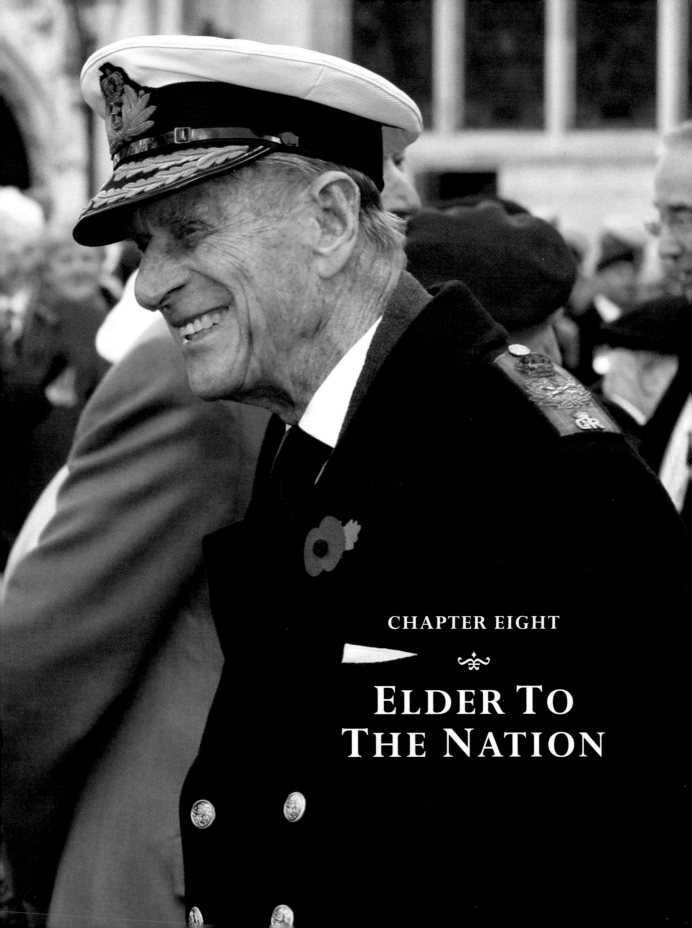

CHAPTER EIGHT

❧

ELDER TO
THE NATION

Mountbatten had had important advice for his great-nephew Charles on the subject of girls. Like countless mentors of upper-class young men, he suggested the sowing of a good many wild oats but the taking of the greatest care in the choice of bride. He happened to have had a candidate in mind – his granddaughter Amanda Knatchbull. He had successfully instigated one royal marriage, so why not another? The couple were fond of each other, but the friendship did not develop. By the early 1980s Mountbatten was gone and Charles was in his thirties – an age when relatives hinted very strongly that he should settle down. Charles himself, comfortable with close friendships he already had, was in no hurry. Philip, who understood and sympathized with a growing public impatience, told his son bluntly that he had better get a move on in finding a wife or there would be no suitable candidates left. Within a short time an eminently acceptable young woman was found in Lady Diana Spencer, the shy but spirited younger sister of one of his former girlfriends. Diana could not hope to match Charles's intellectual interests and she did not care for the causes he championed, but they seemed to like each other and to be comfortable together. Touted throughout his youth as 'the world's most eligible bachelor', Charles's destiny actually made him a very daunting marital prospect, for surprisingly few women in reality relished the lack of privacy and the unrelenting official routine that would have been their lot. Diana Spencer, a nineteen-year-old nursery school assistant whose family was well known to the royals, seemed willing to take on these things, and thus to provide a highly satisfactory companion for him.

She was championed by Philip, who will have seen in her beauty and apparent modesty the potential for a successful consort. He was charming with her, as he has all his life been with women. When Charles dithered, Philip sent him a stiffly worded, old-fashioned letter stating that, having raised both Diana's and the public's expectations, he could not cool their friendship now without badly hurting her feelings and affecting any other marital prospects she might have. Charles allowed himself to be persuaded. The engagement was announced and the marriage went ahead. On the day itself, 29 July 1981, Philip was for much of the service visible to the cameras as he sat near the couple. While he normally looks solemn when in church, he beamed broadly several times as the vows were recited. There was no doubt that he, like the world in general, approved of this match.

As Diana's troubles began, Philip was a source of comfort for her. They corresponded – she addressed him in letters just as his own children did ('Dear Papa') – and he gave her advice on life within the gilded cage of the court. It would be overstating matters to say that they had some sort of special bond, for in the end she would resent him as much as the rest of the family, but there is no question that he did his best to help her acclimatize at least initially, until the preoccupations of her children and her public duties left much less time for this. However difficult she may have found it to fit in both with the family and with their courtiers, her ordeal was mild by comparison with Philip's own introduction to life within 'the Firm'. He remembered his own apprenticeship and he offered what sympathy and understanding he could.

The marriage lasted, as all the world knows, for fifteen years, but by the time the couple divorced it had long been beyond saving. Press photographs had shown an increasingly indifferent body language between Charles and Diana. Then came revelations that both parties had been unfaithful. The damage got worse as supporters of both sides argued in the media. The situation became intolerable, a national and international humiliation. The day after Diana appeared in a television interview, to speak frankly not only about her misery and infidelity but about how much she had disliked her husband's family, the Queen met with the couple and asked them to divorce. There must be damage limitation as soon as possible. It was naturally

TOP RIGHT: The Royal family at Buckingham Palace, London, on the day of Prince William's christening. Standing (from left): the Prince of Wales and Prince Philip; seated (from left): the Queen, the Princess of Wales holding Prince William, and the Queen Mother.

BOTTOM RIGHT: Prince Philip receives a kiss from Diana, Princess of Wales, in London.

LEFT: The Queen and
Prince Philip view the
floral tributes to Diana at
Buckingham Palace.

the Queen, as head of state, who took charge of the situation.

By this time, of course, the whole family was in something of
a state of crisis. Princess Anne had already divorced her husband,
Captain Mark Phillips. And Prince Andrew had parted from his wife,
Sarah, Duchess of York, after less than a decade. Within the space of a
few years the family that had represented the best aspirations of their
people was looking dangerously sordid. Republicans rubbed their
hands. Could the unravelling of these marriages mean the end of the
system? Would they create such widespread disillusionment that the
public would not want them anymore?

The answer was clearly no, but the monarchy had one further
storm to weather before reaching calmer water. In August 1997,
the now emphatically independent Diana was killed in Paris with
her companion Dodi Fayed. The news, predictably, sent shockwaves
around the world. The Royals were at Balmoral when they heard, in
the small hours of a Sunday morning. The first instinct of all the older
members was to protect Diana's two young sons, William and Harry,
from a curious press and public. The way to do this, it was decided,
was to keep their lives as normal as possible. So they attended church
that morning (the sermon made no reference to the tragedy) and
continued stalking during the following days.

The public, which had taken Diana to its heart in the hours
after her death more completely than it had when she was alive,
was furious at what it saw as an indifferent family carrying on as if
nothing had happened. Only after several days, and just in time for
the funeral, did the Queen and Philip travel to London to 'lead the
nation's mourning'. The atmosphere in the crowd as Her Majesty
arrived at Buckingham Palace was one of sullen hostility, but this
melted remarkably quickly as she and her husband began talking
to individuals. She later broadcast to the nation, fully reviving her
popularity. It was her son who was seen as the villain, and he would
go through torments of opprobrium that summer.

The funeral, a public though not a state occasion, brought

hundreds of thousands to line the route. The coffin, accompanied by Welsh Guardsmen, was to pass Buckingham Palace where the family would assemble to acknowledge it before travelling to the Abbey themselves. Diana's brother would be there, as would Charles, Philip and the two Princes. There was some doubt, in this unexpected and unplanned-for situation, as to whether the boys should walk behind the coffin. Philip solved the problem, telling them, 'I'll walk if you will.' The sight of the young men accompanying their father and grandfather was one of the most poignant images of the day.

It is this type of gesture that Philip has always made so well. Throughout the 1990s the Queen was associated in the general consciousness with misfortune, if not outright disaster – there was the Windsor Castle fire, the divorces of her children, and her 'annus horribilis' speech, and then Diana's death. In the twenty-first century the family's public image is more positive. In addition to a new royal wedding and the birth of Prince George, third in line to the throne, the nation has celebrated two jubilees. Though Philip had no public role to play other than simply being in the background, there is no doubt that he will have been of considerable moral support. The Queen has referred to him as 'My rock and stay.' How true that is. The fact that he had to be hospitalized in the midst of the Diamond Jubilee celebrations caused an enormous public concern that reflected his immense popularity.

His charm, when he wishes to exercise it, is unimpaired. When Nicolas Sarkozy, the President of France, came to London on a state visit, his wife, the beautiful and accomplished Carla Bruni, was left to talk to Philip while the two heads of state discussed important matters. She later told interviewers that he had proved to be an archetypal Englishman – amusing and with perfect manners. The same would surely be said by the wives of so many other presidents, prime ministers, ambassadors – the scores, perhaps hundreds, of women (as well as a few men) whom he has had to call upon in their

TOP RIGHT: The Prince of Wales, Prince William, Prince Harry, Earl Spencer and the Duke of Edinburgh walk behind Diana, the Princess of Wales' funeral cortege.

BOTTOM RIGHT: Carla Bruni and Prince Philip share a joke as she and her husband French President Nicolas Sarkozy watch the ceremonial welcome at Windsor Castle with the Queen.

rooms at Buckingham Palace or Windsor and escort to the ballroom
or St George's Hall for a state dinner. As with his speech-making,
constant practice, as well as the vast knowledge he has acquired
through travel and his many varied experiences, must make him one
of the world's great conversationalists.

On his ninetieth birthday in June 2011, the Queen was able to give
her husband a gift that must be of great sentimental value. It was a
title. She created him Lord High Admiral. Despite the Gilbert and
Sullivan sound of this, it is the top of the tree – higher than First Sea
Lord (the height reached by Lord Mountbatten) and First Lord of the
Admiralty. The holder is supreme commander of the Royal Navy, and
it has previously only been held by the monarch. Since she succeeded
her father, Queen Elizabeth had been Lord High Admiral. She made
the position over to her husband not only as a gesture of thanks to a
man who already had virtually every official symbol of recognition,
but as compensation for the career he had sacrificed in the Senior
Service in order to support her. It was a touching – and romantic –
thing to do.

Philip has been portrayed in fiction and in the media for many
years. During the 1980s the satirical television puppet show *Spitting
Image* made considerable fun of his easily caricatured features, his
gravelly voice and even his Greek background. Gentler fun was
poked by Sue Townsend in her book *The Queen and I*, which was later
staged. In this story, the Royal Family are deposed by revolution and
made to live as ordinary people on an urban council estate. While
others adapt, Philip takes to bed and gives up. He features as a minor
character, emerging unshaven in his pyjamas every once in a while
to complain about something. This may raise laughs among a theatre
audience but it is a serious misreading of his character. It is not very
likely that the man so famous for 'just getting on with it' would
buckle under a reverse like that – that the patron of organizations
intended to foster self-confidence and achievement in young people

would himself be found so wanting in initiative; that a man of his reputed bad temper would not hit back out of sheer contrariness — or indeed that closet royalists, of whom there will be some on any council estate, would not lionize their new neighbours and treat them with as much deference as any courtier.

Philip's manner is of course easily lampooned, and writers of comedy have little difficulty putting believable words in his mouth, for his reactions to many situations can be guessed at with varying degrees of accuracy. Regarded as entirely characteristic is a scene from Neil Mackwood and Bryan Rostron's satirical novel *Palace* (1986), in which Philip is stalking in the hills above Balmoral. After a ten-hour pursuit he has the stag in his sights when it suddenly bounds away. The Duke, livid that his day's sport has been ruined, realizes that the animal had caught the scent of approaching humans. Two young men can be seen labouring up the hillside with rucksacks. He strides down to them, demanding to know what they are doing in the area. A survival course, they stammer. He throws his hands up in frustration. 'Ye gods!' he cries, 'What the bloody hell for?'

'The D-duke of Edinburgh's Award S-scheme, Sir,' comes the answer.

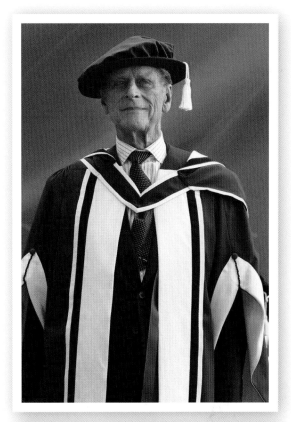

CHAPTER NINE

A LIFETIME OF SERVICE

Prince Philip has had to feel his way in the role that Fate
has assigned him. His private secretary Michael Parker
commented in 1970 that: 'He had to build it up, brick
by brick. I was surprised that he didn't get a great deal of help –
that there wasn't a collection of great men in the land who had
suggestions to make.' Curiously enough, some years later Princess
Diana would complain in similar terms about the lack of guidance
that she received from courtiers, and even from the family itself,
when she entered public life. She found a sympathetic ear in her
father-in-law, Prince Philip, who could remember what it was like to
feel like an outsider.

It has been a considerable gift from Fate, to Great Britain and
to the Commonwealth, that the Queen's husband has been a man
of such qualities. No other could surely have proved so resilient,
so patient, so supportive and yet so dynamic. Accustomed to lead,
he voluntarily accepted a position that was entirely secondary, and
he has maintained it without bitterness or resentment and with
consummate ability. Given very little officially to do, he has found
things for himself that absorb his energies and his enthusiasm, filling
his days with activity that has not only kept him fit but benefited
others. He has raised huge sums for charity through his patronage,
he has popularized causes and products and pastimes through his
links with them. He has done much – probably far more than he is
given credit for – to help the environment and to raise awareness
of the natural world. He has, during more than sixty years, become
the most hardworking and the most extensively travelled member
of the Royal Family ever, though given a similar longevity some
of his children or grandchildren may equal his record. Though his
advancing years have now associated him in the public mind with
'yesterday' rather than today or tomorrow, he has been a most
dynamic symbol of the modern world and has represented a new era
in the history of monarchy.

His wide interests have enabled an unprecedented number of individuals and groups to feel a sense of kinship with him – and have made him, and the institution to which he belongs, relevant. A public that assumed royalty never laugh or tell jokes, never talk to the likes of them, never write their own speeches, never notice those at the back of a crowd, never do their own cooking, never get dirty, never have the intelligence to understand how things work, have never had to earn their own living or go without, and have never suffered personal setbacks or misfortunes, found him a revelation. He was almost like a man of the people who had been elected to office – one of us who had risen to become one of them. He was someone whom men could admire and women could dream about – the nearest thing to a film star that royalty had produced since the Prince of Wales – the man who later became King Edward VIII and then the Duke of Windsor. Any comparison of the two would be absurd. They were utterly, completely different. But while Edward was selfish, shallow and weak, Philip has shown a strength of character and a depth of vision that galvanized much of national life. Edward, after all, entirely lacked Philip's joy in hard work and in worthwhile causes.

If matters had worked out otherwise, what sort of life might he have had as King of Greece? He would have been just as energetic, just as curious and enthusiastic, just as galvanizing, just as generous with his time and trouble. But his country, veering between monarchy and republic, might well have banished him a second time, leaving him to resume the rootless exile that characterized his early years. He may have been foreign by birth, but he fitted so seamlessly into the British way of life that it was somehow unthinkable that he should have been a citizen of any other country, and the older and crustier he has become, the more British he somehow seems. His country of origin, too, would have been too small to provide scope for his energy. Without a Commonwealth to visit, without the panoply of uniforms to wear and the universities and societies and the charities to preside over, it is difficult to imagine him happy;

TOP RIGHT: Prince Philip with a member of the judiciary at the opening of the new Criminal Justice Centre in Manchester, 2009.

BOTTOM RIGHT: The Queen smiles with Prince Philip on Horse Guards Parade during the annual Trooping the Colour parade.

without, even, the 'fundungus' to fight against and to overcome,
he might have found life emptier. Wherever he was he would
have made some sort of mark, and Greece would undoubtedly
have felt the influence of his personality in a thousand ways, but a
small Mediterranean nation whose lifestyle is characterized by an
endearing indifference to urgency does not seem the right setting
for a man with his drive and his demanding nature. Unable to make
progress, he might have given up and gone happily to exile. Britain
was always going to be a country more suited to his talents.

A spectator at one recent event said afterwards, in tones almost
of awe: 'Did you notice how he made eye contact with absolutely
everyone? He didn't just look at us but up at the windows and at the
people at the back who hadn't expected even a distant glance. That
was real professionalism!' Yet it is clear that his famous energy is now
flagging. Ailments visit him more often and his stays in hospital are
more frequent. He has cut back on his public duties, but the fact that
he still carries them out at all, let alone the number of engagements
he fulfils (347 in 2012) is an inspiration. Like the Queen, he does not,
indeed feels he cannot, retire. As she continues to carry out her duties,
so he continues to support her, which is the single thing to which he
has devoted his whole adult life. So he will go on following three paces
behind her in public, and will continue shaking hands and talking to
people in crowds, for as long as he is able to function. He still has
reserves of strength and toughness on which he can draw, and a close
family and medical resources will help. He is now eight years short of
his century – as he might have said in his cricketing days, ninety-two,
not out. One cannot help feeling that there is more to come.